HIRE
BETTER
PEOPLE
FASTER

HIRE
BETTER
PEOPLE
FASTER

A Proven System for Attracting
the Employees You Want

RYAN ENGLIN, JEREMY MACLIVER

HIRE BETTER PEOPLE FASTER
A Proven System for Attracting the Employees You Want

FIRST EDITION

ISBN   978-1-5445-3617-0   *Hardcover*

         978-1-5445-3618-7   *Paperback*

         978-1-5445-3619-4   *Ebook*

         978-1-5445-3620-0   *Audiobook*

CONTENTS

*To all the people we've had the privilege
of hiring over the years,*

*This book is for you. You helped us grow as leaders
and refine this approach to hiring the best—all while inspiring
us to share it with the world. The process we're about to share
would not have been developed without your contributions.
Thank you!*

INTRODUCTION

HIRING BETTER PEOPLE WILL CHANGE YOUR LIFE.

Imagine having a team in which every member not only knows their job, but they do it well. They handle issues before they get to you. And you genuinely trust them to make critical decisions.

Imagine a team that comes up with ideas to make the business better. *They* motivate *you*.

If you had such a team, your growth could skyrocket. You could stop turning away new customers. You'd work normal hours. You'd see your family more. You'd have more time for the things you love.

Your confidence as a leader would rise with your results. Your confidence as a person would increase. And the vision of what your company could achieve would reach previously unimaginable new heights.

You need a team like this, but if you're like most business owners, hiring isn't something you enjoy. Instead, you *struggle through it* to keep the business growing. You wing it. You figure it out when you need to.

Still, in your best moments, you know there has to be a better approach—one that allows you to get the best people in the door.

What if there were a system that could make the whole hiring process simple?

What if that system created an environment in which people were lining up to work with you?

What if you could seek out employees who align with your core beliefs?

What if you could keep the best people long after you hire them?

If you had that kind of system, suddenly that lineup of great employees wouldn't seem like a dream.

Fortunately, this system *isn't* a dream; it's a reality for many business owners. And you deserve that reality, too.

We have experienced this hundreds of times working with businesses that now use the process we share in this book.

One such business is Shelby Erectors, owned by Jack and Jen.

Shelby Erectors is a construction company out of Florida. When we first met Jack, he was working over eighty hours per week. Jen was being dragged into areas of the business she hated. They worked so much it took away from the time they had for their grandkids and their family. Jack was frustrated because he had no time for his favorite pastime: fishing!

Jack and Jen didn't have a bad business. They were experts in their field of building bridges. They had years of experience, a long list of loyal customers, and strong business instincts. The challenge was, they didn't have a team that could make decisions without them. They also didn't have nearly enough skilled workers to complete projects without budget over-runs due to all the overtime. They simply didn't have enough people. They were doing too much themselves. And they had no time to focus on high-level business objectives so the business could grow.

For years, this problem seemed unfixable. Year after year, the company was understaffed and falling short of its potential. Hiring unqualified workers only intensified the problem as they performed less effectively and caused more rework, which generated less profit.

Then, Jack and Jen brought us in.

We are Ryan and Jeremy, experts in hiring better people faster. For both of us, this is more than a career. It's a passion we've had since childhood.

Ryan learned the importance of having the right employees the hard way, watching his father work twelve-hour shifts almost every day of the week while running his own company—all because he never hired the people who could take on some of that responsibility.

Jeremy was born with a mind for efficiency. At age eight, he was helping his mom streamline the household chores process. At nineteen, he hired his first employee out of his own income so he could invest his time more wisely.

Throughout our careers, we've come to specialize. Jeremy focuses on working with leadership teams to create healthy organizations, and Ryan helps companies implement a proven process to attract great employees and hire frontline workers.

That complete perspective on hiring and retaining a team has allowed us to build this process together.

By implementing the system we're about to share, Jack and Jen hired fifty craft workers in ninety days. They restructured their management team to create real accountability.

Fast-forward two years, and the business was hitting record growth and expanding into new territories. Meanwhile, Jack and Jen work a normal thirty-five hours per week.

"It's like being on a permanent vacation," Jack says.

Jack now takes off at two o'clock every Friday afternoon to go fishing on the ocean in his boat, *Steelin' Time*. The couple go mudding with their kids and grandkids every weekend. They travel more too.

Now, fishing might not be your thing. You might have kids and you care about seeing them grow up. Or, you might be nearing retirement, and your business is your nest egg. Whatever your thing is, your inability to hire great people is robbing you of your company's true potential. It's keeping you from the joy and profits that are why you went into business in the first place!

With that possibility in mind, let's do a quick assessment:

- Does your business energize you?

- Do you have a team that you genuinely enjoy working with—one that shares your vision for the company?

- Do the people on your team inspire you?

- Is your business hitting your goals?

- Do you feel it is easy to find good help?

- Do you have the confidence to hold people accountable because you know you can replace them if you have to?

If you answer "no" to any of those questions, you're reading the right book. This is the book that can transform all those "nos" to "yeses," allowing you to create an energized, aligned, and inspiring team that consistently hits your goals.

That potential is within reach. People problems are a straightforward fix. The system you learn here will turn your business into a magnet for the workers you need. And when you hire better, every other business problem gets easier to fix.

When hiring is easy, you create a sustainable, growing business powered by an incredible team.

THE CORE FIT HIRING SYSTEM

Jack and Jen, and every other entrepreneur you read about in this book, transformed their business with the Core Fit Hiring System. The Core Fit Hiring System is a set of tools and practices to help you hire better people faster. And when we say "better people" what we really mean is the type of workers who are so aligned with your vision they will do anything to help you achieve it. Hiring these people will expand your business in ways you can't fathom.

To do this, we'll follow seven steps that will allow you to attract, hire, and retain top talent:

- **Core**: where you strategically define and share your company vision, purpose, and values. It's the foundation of your employer brand and the story you'll share to attract the right people.

- **Find**: the first external step, where you get strategic about getting in front of the people you need.

- **Automate**: removing the time-consuming parts of recruitment so you can focus on what's most important in hiring.

- **Interview**: how you discover the right people and eliminate those who aren't a good fit.

- **Onboard**: get the first ninety days right, and you'll have the start of a trusting relationship with a highly motivated employee—and far less turnover.

- **Engage**: how you improve productivity and make more money without a lot of effort, all while motivating people to stay longer.

- **Assess**: how you improve, adapt, and iterate your recruiting process to stay with the times.

With all these steps in place, you can create a cycle in which you hire better people who stick around longer and are continuously improving the experience for all.

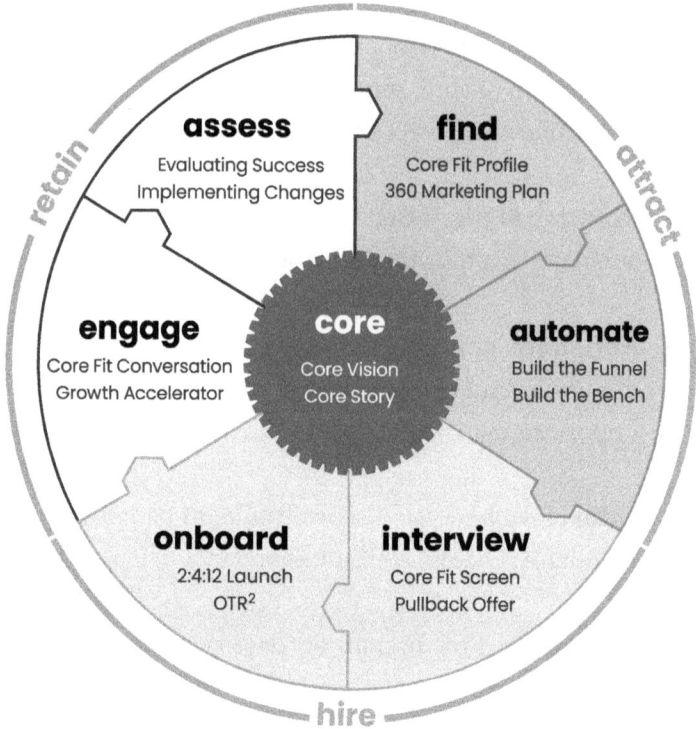

retain

assess
Evaluating Success
Implementing Changes

find
Core Fit Profile
360 Marketing Plan

attract

engage
Core Fit Conversation
Growth Accelerator

core
Core Vision
Core Story

automate
Build the Funnel
Build the Bench

onboard
2:4:12 Launch
OTR^2

interview
Core Fit Screen
Pullback Offer

hire

HIRING DOESN'T HAVE TO BE HARD

We hear all the time, "Hiring is hard." Owners say, "It's a pain," or, "Let's just outsource it." But anything in business is painful when you don't have a process. This book gives you a proven process—The Core Fit Hiring System—to avoid the "pain" of hiring. It's time to make hiring a nonissue so you can attract the people you need, win in business, and get your life back.

1

HIRING DOESN'T HAVE TO BE HARD

I struggled for years to expand our customer base. No matter who I brought in, no one seemed to connect with the customers. That responsibility always came back to me. I had to make the calls, knock on the doors, and handle the follow-ups. I had to sign new customers if I wanted to keep the business growing.

Then, I hired Claire. Within a month, I knew I had someone special. Within six months, she was selling ten times as much as the next salesperson.

How did she do it? I asked Claire to take some notes on her tactics.

In typical Claire fashion, she did so much more than that. She reviewed the entire sales process and showed the whole company what wasn't working. Then, she mapped out how her changes could improve sales—for everyone.

She single-handedly transitioned the company to new best habits, raised sales across the organization, and freed up so much of my time.

—MARY, owner of a housecleaning company in Florida

* * *

I wasn't sure about Erik at first. We'd just changed our hiring process, and he was the first candidate I interviewed. On paper, he wasn't ideal. He wasn't fully certified yet, and I had already seen a long list of techs with better qualifications fall short of what I needed.

But I followed the process, and Erik won me over during the interview. He was so passionate about the work. When I mentioned I wanted to expand, he was eager to talk about the part he could play in that process.

I'd never heard that before. So, I hired him.

Two months later, he was fully certified and the best performer on my team. It's been five years now, and Erik is overseeing our entire expansion project.

—SEBASTIAN, owner of an HVAC company in Wisconsin

* * *

For many years, I prided myself on running the day-to-day operations of the company. I loved being in charge of every aspect of the work. But I was getting older, and I didn't want to spend my retirement years handling customer complaints and dealing with the backlog of service tickets.

I looked around the office, and I didn't see anyone who could step up. I began to feel depressed. Maybe I would have to keep working until I died—whether I liked it or not.

Nate saved my golden years. I hired him when a competitor foolishly let him leave instead of giving him more responsibility. He's now my lead tech and puts out every fire in the organization.

Before Nate, I was working sixty hours a week. Now, I'm down to thirty. And by the end of this year, I'm retiring.

—DAVID, owner of an electrical contractor in Pennsylvania

* * *

Looking across your organization and recent hires, you might assume you simply can't find the kind of people that helped transform these organizations. As far as many business owners are concerned, these stories might as well be fiction.

But there are Claires, Eriks, and Nates all over the place, and plenty of them would eagerly work for your company. You just need a proven system to find them and convince them to work for you.

Great employees are out there.

They will transform your organization—and your life.

The model and tools we will share with you in this book can resolve this problem. They work for every company but are designed for companies between ten and five hundred employees—particularly companies that hire a lot of frontline workers. These business owners love their people and love their work, but they also want to love their lives. That requires hiring the best people.

The Core Fit Hiring System works for companies who hire a lot of frontline workers. These jobs take a lot of grit, determination, consistency, and reliability. They aren't always the most popular jobs. Flextime and remote work environments often aren't practical. This book, this model, and these tools have been carefully designed over the past ten years to help leaders create the team they need to serve their customers, grow the business, and free up their time.

WHERE DID ALL THE GOOD WORKERS GO?

Business owners come to us out of frustration. They're tired, they're overworked and strained to the breaking point—and they can't seem to hire anyone able to help. They're so frustrated, they've almost convinced themselves that great employees don't exist anymore. At least, not for them.

We tell these owners that the job market is stocked with great people. And they want to work for a company like yours.

The challenge is that the employment market has been slowly shifting, while hiring practices remain stagnant.

To find good workers, you have to change how you look at hiring. To do that, you need to look at what shifted.

Technology

Technology has played a big part in the hiring transition. Google, hiring apps, social media, and job boards give applicants the ability to see a lot more options than before. Job seekers can be more selective. They can compare across a much larger pool of opportunities, even expanding it well past where they live. To win in the hiring game, you will have to win in technology.

More Options

This one can feel very defeating for many teams. Most of the companies we work with are hiring a lot of frontline workers with set schedules. The work can be hard and labor intensive. The gig economy and work-from-home jobs are your competition.

When you hire an electrician, a customer service representative, or a line cook for a restaurant, the ads right next to yours offer work-from-home jobs. Or flextime. Or some other employee perk that isn't possible in your industry. If you ignore this, you will struggle to hire. In no way are we saying that you must offer these, and in fact, many of the teams we see can't offer these. You must be aware of them, and you must make an offering that is attractive enough to keep them moving in your direction.

Time Commitment

In a world of instant gratification, applying and hiring decisions can feel like they take a lot of time. To further complicate the issue, you may have one timeline that feels right for you, while applicants are running on a different level of expectancy—after all, they have bills to pay. Large corporations have recognized this and learned ways to stay connected with the applicant in a fast and efficient time frame. You probably feel you don't have the time or money to fully dedicate the attention needed to keep up. There are solutions available, but to overcome this, you can't ignore them.

New Expectations in the Workplace

People have changed their view of work.

While entrepreneurs and business leaders continue to look at employees through a simple equation of time + labor = pay, workers today want something more. We live in a world that is both more connected and more isolated than ever. People feel alone, and they can see others feel that way too.

Employees now expect work to provide what's missing.

People want to feel like they belong. They want to feel like they're valued. Money is still important, but if all you provide is money, your people will look for alternatives.

If you can't offer dedicated leadership, a culture they believe in, and a team they want to be a part of, they'll look elsewhere.

And if you do have dedicated leaders, an amazing culture, and great people already on the team, you have to make sure people know it. After all, as a small business, if you don't scream it from the mountaintops, no one will notice.

Take Taddiken Tree Company in Boulder, Colorado, for example. They have a fun company culture and committed ownership, but their job ads got mixed up with all the other job postings.

Recognizing the need for change, Taddiken transformed its hiring process and increased employee retention by integrating their values and humor into their job advertisements. This new approach successfully attracted better candidates who resonated with the company culture.

By showcasing their company's unique identity, they were able to stand above the rest and bring the best new hires in.

WHY CHANGE THIS NOW?

For all the trouble you've had with hiring, you've gotten by. So why change now?

Honestly? You're running out of time.

In the early 2000s, newspapers thought they could keep getting by. The internet was claiming readership, but many refused to change. Those papers went out of business. The ones that remain are the ones that were most eager to adapt.

We work with hundreds of companies a year, helping them pivot to new practices that allow them to recruit, hire, and retain the best employees out there. If you don't make that pivot soon, your competitors will. And they'll have a decisive advantage over you.

This issue isn't going to go away. Whatever changes are happening, people fundamentally want something different from their job than they used to. You've got to provide it, and you've got to advertise it. If you don't, then employees—good and bad—will flow in and out, at a faster and faster speed. This turnover happens because the alternative is simply unsustainable.

Ryan recently had a call with the president of a franchise company with 130 locations. He told Ryan about some data he'd unearthed.

"The average company size is five employees," he said. "Do you know how many W-2s the average company issued last year?

"It certainly isn't five. It isn't twenty-five, either. It's forty-one."

Employees—good and bad—are flowing in and out of jobs these days because companies like yours don't know how to find the right people, encourage them to apply, hire them, and keep them happy.

If you don't change now, this will keep getting harder. If your competitors wise up sooner than you, they'll keep hiring all the Claires, Eriks, and Nates in your area. And you? You'll be creating a job for yourself that you'll have to work at for the rest of your life—because you can't find anyone else to do it.

Some business owners who come to us make the call because they wake up at sixty and realize they can't retire. They can't step back because no one can take over. They can't sell because the business barely exists without them.

They've been incredibly successful and built remarkable businesses, but they're trapped in a job that won't give them a weekend off for the rest of their lives.

And it's all because they didn't hire well.

It's time to change that for you.

Fortunately, we're here to help.

DEFINE YOUR STRATEGY

Another reason hiring is so hard for most business owners is that they don't have a defined strategy or process. This has been the case for a very long time, but with all of the changes in how an applicant views the process, it is now a serious liability. You must have a strategy or process to win.

Whether you believe it or not, there are good people ready and willing to work for you. These same people will free you from this cycle and give you a business that leaves you rested, confident, and energized. So let's get started.

To overcome the hiring challenges we've already discussed, you need to choose your strategy. There are three main ways to recruit great people into your company:

- Hunting

- Farming

- Fishing

All three of these strategies are useful, and you should employ all of them in your organization. But only one is unique in its ability to get you high-quality people whenever you need them without investing more time and money into the process. Now, let's take a look at each.

Hunting

Hunting is the hiring practice of seeking out, or recruiting, the one ideal candidate for a particular job. Instead of waiting for applicants to come to you, you decide on who you want to hire and you go hunting for them.

The challenge is that hunting can be quite expensive and time consuming. It requires precise planning, dedication, and an ongoing investment. Because you're hiring for one position at a time, hunting can never stop. If your organization is hungry, you have to keep hunting.

For that reason, most organizations that rely on hunting have to either outsource the process or create dedicated positions to constantly do it.

For companies with a number of frontline employees, this is unsustainable. Hunting should be reserved for filling your top positions. When you need a new executive or a new specialist, you should go hunting. For the vast majority of your workforce, though, it's inefficient.

Farming

If hunting isn't getting results, farming is often where companies turn. This is the process of cultivating the talent you already have and raising them up to meet your future needs.

Apprenticeships, training programs, working with colleges and high schools—these are all forms of farming. These can all provide promising individuals with a pathway to growth in your organization.

Unfortunately, farming can take years to show results. It isn't going to improve your workforce quickly. And that's a problem when you need to improve that workforce now.

You also take on some risk when relying exclusively on farming. If you invest in training your team for the next six months and half that team leaves, that wastes time and effort. And then you have to start all over.

Farming is a perfect strategy when you already have a team of good workers. Turning good workers into top performers and your future leaders is a valuable long-term aim. But you need that good team to be in place first.

Fishing

Last summer, Ryan went deep-sea fishing for the first time. He knew nothing about the process. He chartered a boat, and he put his faith in the captain.

For three hours, the captain sailed around until he found a spot where he knew the fish would bite. Then, he gave Ryan some bait, showed him how to put it on the tackle, and left Ryan to cast his line.

Ryan caught two mahi-mahi that day.

That doesn't mean that Ryan was suddenly an expert, but with minimal effort, he had some immediate, significant results.

That's what fishing has to offer. Once you understand the process, fishing is a fast, inexpensive way to get real results. It doesn't take a huge investment or constant focus.

Find a good spot; cast a line; catch some fish. It's that simple.

So, what is fishing?

This is the process of going to where the best candidates are, putting out the right bait, and letting them nibble at the hook. You don't hunt them. You don't farm them from within the organization. They come to you ready and eager to do the job because they *want* the job, and they *want* to work for you.

This is the best way to stock an entire organization with better workers. It's cheaper, faster, and more effective on a large scale than farming and hunting. It's low risk, and it doesn't require a whole department or outsourcing.

For all these reasons, it will be the focus of the rest of this book.

Once we have you fishing, you can throw your hook in the water, walk away, and come pull a fish out of the water as soon as you need one.

And when you do this right, the fish on that hook isn't a minnow. It's a bluefin tuna. It is exactly the person you need to transform your company.

A MODERN HIRING SYSTEM

When you need to hire for frontline positions—those that provide your product or service to your customers or interact directly with them—you often need more people than hunting or farming can provide. That is why fishing is the ideal solution for any company struggling to hire and willing to do things differently.

Don't go ordering fishing poles and tackle, though. Fishing is really just using the right tools to attract the best people for the job and retaining them long after hire. We've seen this process work across many industries and in every region in this country. It can work for your company, too.

The ideas ahead have transformed companies into elite hiring organizations with teams filled with Claires, Eriks, and Nates.

To join their ranks, you will need a system that can cut through the obstacles in the current job market and bring you the best candidates. Or rather, you'll need *the* system: the Core Fit Hiring System.

2

CORE

We were up on the rooftops, taking fire. The shots were coming out of the dark near the village. It was twelve Green Berets against a determined enemy and without any chance of support.

We took a collective deep breath and prepared for another long night.

It was the spring of 2005, and we were outside a remote village in Afghanistan. Our team had all signed up for one reason: we believed in going to places that most of the world had forgotten and helping those who had been left behind.

Our mission was to make a connection with the farmers in this region, build some relationships, and empower these people to fight back.

It wasn't easy. The people in this village had endured forty years of endless war. They had low trust with each other, let alone with a group of outsiders like us.

Complicating things further, we were surrounded by the Taliban on all sides. Every night, they attacked.

As we settled in for another rough and dangerous night, we heard shots fired from another direction. We looked around to see if the Taliban had taken another position. But no, it was one of the farmers. He was standing on his roof. And he was firing at the Taliban.

That's when I knew we'd won the battle for the hearts of those villagers. Once someone gets up on their roof like that, they've made the calculation that they want to defend your life as much as their own. They've made the commitment to join forces with you.

He was by no means the last to join us. Our mission started in six villages that had seventy-five farmers between them. Within eighteen months, the Green Berets had expanded to 113 villages and created 38,000 fighters.

That's the power of great leadership. Once you've shown someone who you really are, if they decide to follow, they'll follow you anywhere.

—SCOTT MANN, author and former Green Beret

You can build a team as dedicated as the one Scott Mann and his team assembled in Afghanistan. Your company can inspire loyalty, dedication, and creativity across your workforce.

You can get these results—if you build from the core of who you really are. As Scott said, at that point, "if they decide to follow, they'll follow you anywhere."

To do this, you need to hire from your Core. Your Core is what your business is built upon. It's the values, vision, purpose, and story that make your company unique. After all, you aren't running ACME Generic, LLC. If you want your team to be invested enough to follow you anywhere, you need to define how you are unique in each of these components:

1. **Core Values**: This is how the team should operate. It outlines the critical behaviors that will make your team strong and able to achieve the company's goals.

2. **Core Vision**: This is the roadmap for where you're going. It's the big-picture destination you want people to get behind.

3. **Core Purpose**: This drives you and your team to overcome obstacles. It is why they get out of bed to fight for you.

4. **Core Story**: This is the story you tell about your values, vision, and purpose to your employees, customers, and the world.

When you hire people that align with your Core, they'll be more excited, more engaged, more productive, and ultimately more profitable. To bring in the best people and get the most from them, you must inspire them to believe in you and your company. And that means you have to strengthen each component of your Core.

CORE VALUES

Core Values define the way you operate. They outline the critical behaviors that will make your team strong and able to achieve the company's goals.

We've had leaders tell us core values are fluffy, stuffy, and stupid. It's true, core values *can be* fluffy and stupid—if they're done *wrong*. But that's not what Core Values are. You do not create Core Values. They come *from within* you.

In other words, your Core Values are already in place. Your job is to simply bring them out into the open and state them clearly for your employees and your customers.

Your Core is all about authenticity. This was key to the success of Scott Mann's Green Beret team in Afghanistan. Scott was able to create a bond with the villagers by honestly sharing his values and his experiences. He grew up on a farm, and he knew the values required to keep a farm running: hard work, dedication, and fortitude.

Because he shared those values, the villagers saw not a man in uniform from another country but a fellow traveler who understood them: a person they could trust to lead them.

We know that many entrepreneurs are skeptical of Core Values. Adam, the owner of AIS, thought this entire exercise was pointless.

"I'm not a touchy-feely guy," he told us. "I don't need this touchy-feely values stuff, and I don't understand why anyone else would want it."

This is a common response from frustrated leaders because they can't find good people. The people they have don't behave like the business leader thinks they should. And the reason for this is they haven't discovered and defined their Core Values.

Core Values come naturally from you, the business owner, so while you may not need to see them on a wall, your team does.

It can feel unnecessary to write them out because you already behave in alignment with your values. But your team doesn't know that. Your Core Values must be named so your team can align too.

When your team is built around your Core Values, there's a relationship of mutual trust. You trust your people to behave in line with the company's best interest, and they trust you to behave in a way that speaks to their values too.

Core Values are about planting your flag. It's telling the world who you are as an organization. With clear Core Values, you can set your standards and attract those who believe in them.

With Adam, all we had to do was observe him and his team. Just watching everyone interact, we could see the values already on display.

When we presented those values to Adam, he was blown away.

"That's exactly us!"

A few weeks later, in a coaching session, Adam admitted, "I know this wasn't something I wanted to do at first, but I totally understand why we needed this. Now, everyone knows what we stand for."

This is about defining who you are and finding people who want to share that definition. And when those people join your organization, you know they'll follow you anywhere.

What Makes a Core Value?

Your company's Core Values should fit six criteria:

1. Clear

2. Actionable

3. Unique

4. Supported by Real Life Examples

5. Motivational

6. Five or Fewer

Core Values have to be **clear**. Clarity means people immediately understand what your Core Values mean. You can spell them out in simple language. After all, if people don't understand what you mean, how will you attract people who align with them?

If you value safety, focus on what safety means to you, perhaps, "taking care of people." "Teamwork" can mean many things, whereas "winning together" is much clearer. And "integrity" might lead to different interpretations, but not "following through on promises."

Similarly, each value should be **actionable**. You'll eventually measure people's alignment with your values based on what they do and how they act. If you can't see them in action, they can't be implemented, followed, and measured.

A Core Value could also be a mindset. For example, we worked with a client with a Core Value of "No Can'ts." This isn't an action, necessarily, but it's fairly straightforward what is expected and how you should measure it. "No Can'ts" is about finding a solution when the obvious solution isn't present. If an employee is walking around saying "I can't" do something, they're not the right person for the company.

One component of Core Values that is often overlooked is that they are meant to be **unique**. They are how you differentiate yourself, rise above others, and stand out from the crowd.

You can have a set of Core Values similar to another company in your industry, but you never want to replicate their list. This list is about *you*. They're *your* values.

In his book *Purple Cow*, marketing expert Seth Godin states that the old way to build a business (making safe, average products and then marketing them by buying as much TV advertising you can afford) is no longer effective. Instead, we need to make remarkable products that customers will tell other people about. He urges businesses that to stand out, "they have to be a purple cow in everything they do." This same logic holds true for your Core Values. Unique Core Values will get you noticed. They will be different enough that everyone picks you out of a field full of job opportunities.

Your values also need to be **supported by real-life examples**. You need to have stories to share about your team living out your Core Values. These stories work together with the **motivational** aspect of your Core Values. You can have everything else right and see values fall flat if they don't motivate your whole team.

When we worked with All Things Metal, they did all the right things to document their values. Still, owner Timothy Rock found that those values weren't resonating because they weren't motivational.

That's when Timothy read *Rhinoceros Success* by Scott Alexander. In the book, Alexander points out the qualities that the rhino possesses: commitment, dedication, and single focus. These were qualities that Timothy valued and shared, but reading about the rhino helped him visualize these values and bring them to life. He wanted the values at All Things Metal to have the same impact.

So we helped him change up the language to add a little inspiration and motivation to those values. Now, the company pursued the value of "Rhinoceros Dedication."

That little extra inspiration allowed Timothy to attract better people. His workers were excited to compare themselves to the mighty rhino. Rhinoceros pictures appeared all over the office.

With results like that, you might want to throw every possible value into your Core Values list, but that response is only possible with a few key values. In fact, you want your list of Core Values to have **five or fewer** values on it.

Your Core Values need to be memorable. They also need to sink in. Workers should be able to absorb each value, connect it to their own value set, and see that value in their work. That's hard to do if the list is long—so keep it short.

This also forces you to discipline yourself and find those values that really speak to your Core.

Listing Potential Values

To discover your Core Values, break down three areas where your values play a prominent role in your life:

1. Your business

2. Your personal life

3. Your relationships

Brainstorm a list of values for each of these areas. It may help to consider the qualities you admire in other people. What values do you admire in a mentor who helped you achieve your dreams? What values did you appreciate in the best employee you've ever had? What values do you look for in friends?

Do you look for loyalty, dedication, and pride in your work above all else? Or are you more focused on family, supporting one another, and resilience in the face of difficulty?

At this point, write down every value that comes to mind. Once you have a complete list, you can narrow it down. Begin this process by combining similar values. For example, if you have "integrity" and "they always do what they say" on your list, combine them.

Sorting Your Values

With your values grouped together, you can concentrate on eliminating those values that aren't actually core to who you are and what your company stands for. Remember you're only looking for three to five.

According to business management expert and author of *The Advantage*, Patrick Lencioni, there are four types of values. The primary ones are Core Values. The other three are:

1. Accidental values

2. Permission-to-play values

3. Aspirational values

None of these three categories should make your Core Values list.

Accidental Values Can Divide

Accidental values come about unintentionally without considering the team or business needs. For this reason, they're often difficult to identify as such. They've accidentally become the norm.

These values aren't necessarily good or bad, but they do have the potential to divide your team or limit your company's potential.

In his book, Lencioni talks about a company specializing in fashion accessories that only hired young hipsters. It's easy to see how such a value could creep into a creative company. However, hiring along those standards caused problems. Job seekers who weren't in the demographic felt alienated. Many felt discouraged from applying, and those who did get a position felt they didn't belong. The company accidentally decreased its pool of good talent.

We once worked with an electrical contractor. One day a group of people from the company were in our office, and we noticed something they all had in common. They all had massive tattoos, a clear accidental value of the team.

When we asked about this commonality, they were surprised. It was only then that the group realized they didn't spend much time with people who didn't value body art. Digging into their employment history, they found that whenever they hired someone without tattoos, they rarely worked out. It wasn't until they recognized this accidental value that they could work on removing it from their hiring process.

Accidental values aren't always physical or superficial. They might involve a certain type of humor, communication styles, or interests. Essentially, business owners hire people similar to them, even when those similarities aren't important for the job being filled.

Removing accidental values allows you to hire based on the values that actually matter.

Permission-to-Play Values Are Just the Beginning

According to Lencioni, permission-to-play values do not need to be stated because they are the table stakes. Frankly, you shouldn't be allowed in business if you don't have them.

We refer to permission-to-play values as societal values because they are dictated by society. You don't need to explain them, and you shouldn't be hiring people who violate them. They also aren't Core Values. Everyone everywhere should follow these standards. They don't differentiate your culture from the rest, and you don't need to call them out.

A popular example is honesty. If you have to remind an employee not to steal, you likely made a hiring mistake. Respect for property isn't a Core Value because that's the baseline.

You see these values everywhere: quality work, trustworthiness, and safety. These are important values, but they aren't your values; they're every business's values.

If you feel very passionate about a permission-to-play value, ask yourself if you're really behaving differently than others. If you aren't, it's permission to play and not a Core Value.

Aspirational Values Are Nice to Have

In an article for *Harvard Business Review*, Lencioni said of aspirational values, "Most value statements are bland, toothless, or just plain dishonest...empty values statements create cynical and dispirited employees, alienate customers, and undermine managerial credibility."

For this reason, it is important for you to be real with yourself and with your values list. Which values reflect the truth about who you are and what your business represents—and which ones reflect what you *wish* was true of yourself and your business?

One of our clients once told us he valued tidiness while sitting at a messy conference table. Tidiness was undoubtedly a value he *wanted*, but he didn't live that way.

If a Core Value is on your list, be sure it represents how you and your team actually behave. Otherwise, you devalue everything you say as a business.

To attract and keep the best employees, you and your company have to embody your values. You want to tell people precisely what you stand for and attract people who agree.

That doesn't mean you can't aim for improvement, but aspiration is, by definition, not core to who you are.

So look around your workplace, ask a team member, or simply look in the mirror. If that value isn't deeply rooted in everything you do, it isn't part of your Core. And it doesn't make your Core Values list.

Values in Your Own Words

With a better understanding of the four types of values, you're now ready to finalize your Core Values list into those three to five principles that provide the foundation for all you do. It's likely that values on your list have generic names, like "team" or "family." Take that idea and state it in a way that speaks to your Core.

Here is how three different clients got more specific on what "Team" means to them:

- **"Together in Excellence**—We're better because we are a team, and we create excellence because we are part of that team. We are always looking for ways to improve and to rise up together."

- **"Invest in Each Other**—We 'walk in their shoes' and value the whole person. We lead with empathy to build a healthy team."

- **"Share the Foxhole**—We must appreciate and respect the whole person. And until we've walked in someone's shoes, we can't pretend to know what they're going through. We're a member of the community we serve and we remain connected to each and every one of our customers."

Whether it's "team," "customer service," or "quality work," find your own unique way to speak to this value. It will make the

Core Value more memorable, while also showing that it truly comes from you.

Communicating Your Core Values

Your list is now five or fewer items. They are unique to you and your organization. It's time to concentrate on making the language clear, straightforward, and motivational while adding real-world examples.

This requires a certain amount of creative finesse and personality. For instance, if "Interdependent Problem-Solver" is a value, that terminology needs to be used by everyone all the time. If the team always comes together to solve a problem, ask yourself, "Are we being interdependent problem-solvers?"

Use the Core Values words repeatedly to reinforce them in yourself and your team. Repetition makes them part of who you are. You are not going to overdo this. We worked with a client that at the beginning of every team meeting had everyone recite their Core Values.

That repetition is important—because these are *your* values. However, this isn't the only component of your Core. A business isn't just about its values, it also has a clear direction of where it's going.

Now that you have values to guide today, it's time to set your course.

CORE VISION

To create a great team, you will have to articulate your goals so you can attract the people who share them.

That is the ultimate aim of your vision: to get the best people into your company and make that vision possible. Business management expert Jim Collins, in his book *Good to Great*, argues, "People who build great organizations make sure they have the right people on the bus."

In other words, vision without great people is irrelevant. And the inverse is also true. Just having great people isn't enough.

After all, if you want to attract the right people to join your company, you need to give them clarity on where the company is going. That means you have to be clear on the destination first. And that requires a clear Core Vision for the entire operation.

Jim Collins, author of *Good to Great*, uses the metaphor of your business being like a bus. Your job, according to Collins, is to get the right people on your bus, in the right seat, and all excited about the destination. To do that, your Core Vision has to come before you load a great team onto the bus. Otherwise, the second there's a problem—and there will be problems—they're off. Any flat tires, heavy traffic, or change in the itinerary, and they'll be off hailing down someone else for a ride.

People want to be going *somewhere*. They want to be excited about what is down the road for them. Consider the difference it makes to those bus passengers if they know the destination is a ski resort in the mountains. They would only get on if they really wanted to go there. And once they're on, they're much more likely to stay on the bus through delays because they are excited about the destination.

And the clearer you can make that destination, the more the people on the bus want to stay. As Gino Wickman explains in his book *Traction,* you need to paint a picture of what it looks like.

If you're taking everyone skiing, there's more power in describing what they will see once they get there. Will there be snow falling? Beautiful trees? An epic view of a valley? Painting the picture will be more effective than simply naming the location.

You need to be able to communicate your Core Vision in a way that everyone around you can "see" it.

That way, everyone can see where you're heading.

Vision Shows Who Can Be Great

Imagine you're scheduled to speak to a group of people who are all interested in hiking. The first thing you need to do is set a location, and you've decided to take on the ultimate adventure:

climbing Mount Everest. When you propose the trip, you paint a picture of what is ahead: the scale of the task and the majestic reward.

After you finish, you look around for a show of hands. You quickly notice three camps in the room. There's the not-for-me group who were looking for a nice hike in a nearby forest. Then, there are the fence-sitters. This group wants more adventurous destinations, but most will ultimately decide this is too much. Finally, you have your adventure enthusiasts. These are people who have already conquered Mount Kilimanjaro, and they want to take on the highest peak. "Sign me up," they shout.

Your immediate instinct may be disappointment. After all, you want everyone on this trip. But in reality, your vision has done its job. You've created a clear destination. Now, it's up to people to opt in or out for themselves.

Imagine climbing Mount Everest with a group of hikers who don't want to go. Every day, along with all the tough climbing, you must deal with complaints and grumbling. *Do we have to get up that early? Do we have to work that hard? How much do I get paid for this?* By the time you get to Base Camp 1, most of them have given up and gone back down the mountain. You're now carrying more load, and you've just reduced your chance of successfully reaching the summit.

Whereas, if you have a group of ambitious trekkers who have completely bought into the journey ahead, you have a team ready to do whatever it takes to make sure everyone reaches the peak. They come up with ideas on how to make the trip more successful. They overcome obstacles before you even hear about them.

If you don't have people who want to go where you do, it will feel like you're dragging them up a hill. Dragging people uphill is a problem at the best of times, but it's far worse when obstacles get in your way. As the climbing gets tougher and the weather more unforgiving, you can't afford to pull others up the mountain.

Teams with a clearly defined vision are resilient and focused. The team moves like an unshakable force through any storm. They might pause and assess how conditions have changed, but they continue to look for ways to climb a little higher each day.

That's the power of your Core Vision. It allows the team to build itself, and once the team is in place, it drives them. It gives the team meaning.

Perspective is everything. A bricklayer could be laying bricks or building a church. In the first instance, this is just a job with no meaning beyond the paycheck. In the second, this work has real meaning. There's a big difference.

So if you want those bricklayers saving the world or that team climbing Everest, you will need to create a Core Vision that brings that team together.

Defining Your Core Vision

To develop a Core Vision is deceptively simple. You cast your eye ten years into the future and describe what you see. The biggest mistake that business owners make with vision, though, is that they focus on their ten-year business goals. They make everything about market share, shareholder value, or profitability. These components are important, but they are things only the owners and investors of the company care about.

When an employee is two, three, or five levels removed from the owner, it's really hard for them to get excited about future profitability or a new product. What does that have to do with them? What's in it for them?

The question you have to answer is why *they* should care about where *your* company is going.

Your vision has to answer that question.

That doesn't mean you have to change where you want the company to go—you just have to connect that destination to the people in your company.

Most of the members of your team don't understand that when the company's profitability goes up, you are going to reinvest in the business. And if they are a big part of the business, guess what? That means *you* are reinvesting in *them*. The link between your business goals and their success is there, you just have to show it to them.

We have one construction company client who just recently graduated from our program. His vision states that every single employee, customer, and person that their work touches will have a story to tell about how their *personal* life was impacted by that company.

The power of this vision is that the company was already creating these stories. They were just putting it on paper now. That vision inspired the team. Everyone wanted to have a story. Everyone realized that the company intended to invest in them, making them want to invest in the company.

The company didn't come up with this vision out of thin air. Originally, their vision was about the same revenue and business goals we've all heard before. By stretching just a little, though, they found something people could really connect to. Instead of increasing market share, they realized they wanted to make a bigger impact. They wanted to change people's lives for the better.

As you dig into your own motivations and seek the perspective that shows your teams what is in it for them, keep in mind that you have to prioritize clarity. You want your vision to be clear enough that you could walk up to a janitor on your team and say, "Here's the vision for the company," and that janitor would buy in. They want to get on the bus. And once they're on, they want to stay there.

So, where is your bus going? And why do the people on your bus want to keep riding it? As you begin to think about that point ten years in the future, consider not just what you want to achieve as a business but what actually got you here in the first place—and what will get you the rest of the way.

Your vision can focus on many different things. We've found that some of the most powerful address core concerns of your people: security, longevity, and peace of mind.

Do you want to create a company in which your employees can go home at the end of each workday and be confident that their job is going to be there tomorrow? Do you want a company built upon a sense that every boss knows the value of their team?

Sometimes the motivation behind a vision can be more intangible. Ask yourself (or your team) what they care about in their work. Do they want to be the best? Do they want this to be the best workplace in the region? Do they want individual recognition? Do they want to make an impact on the world?

Or you could take a different angle and focus on education and training. Most people want some kind of training or personal development.

The vision for one company we worked with was that every single employee could retire as a millionaire. They brought in expert financial advisors. They brought in Dave Ramsey's Financial Peace University and Smart Dollar Budgeting. They brought these things in to teach these people how to take care of their money, how to invest their money, and how to save for the future so that they could retire millionaires.

Imagine how excited your team would be about a vision like that.

Now, it's easy to draw people toward the more financially focused vision you have for the company. Your people want to retire millionaires. For that to happen, though, the company has to grow. It has to increase its market share. It has to bring in new revenue and become more profitable.

Suddenly, your vision isn't a piece of paper on the wall about financial goals that only affect the owner and investors. Everyone sees the part they must play in making that growth a reality.

Then, all you have to do is make sure you live up to the promise of that vision.

CORE PURPOSE

People don't just want to go to work to clock in, fill their required hours, and leave with a paycheck. They want their work to mean something. They want to work for you because your company has a real purpose.

For that reason, it's important to take that general sense of purpose and distill it into a clear and concise statement that explains the company's reason for existing to everyone.

Defining Your Core Purpose

Your Core Purpose is a statement that speaks to why you do what you do. If your Core Values explain how you behave and your Core Vision speaks to where you are going, your Core Purpose says why you get out of bed every morning to do what you're doing.

This goes beyond the surface-level, immediate answers that come to mind. For instance, on some level, every business exists to make money. But we don't believe that money is ever the central motivator for an entrepreneur.

For example, we need blood to live, but the meaning of life isn't blood. Money is the blood of the business, and sometimes owners struggle to identify the true purpose of the business. What is driving them to keep the business blood moving?

Money is nice, but it isn't your—or your team's—primary motivator. You could probably make more money and invest less of your time with other businesses. There's something deeper here, and to get at it, you have to ask a very simple question: why?

Simon Sinek, the author of *Start with Why*, is famously known for saying, "People don't buy WHAT you do; they buy WHY you do it."

Sinek further clarifies that a good *why* answers, "WHY does your company exist? WHY do you get out of bed every morning? And WHY should anyone care?"

This is a big task for one statement, but it's possible to pack a lot into a few words. For example, at Core Matters, our purpose statement is:

"Our company exists to help entrepreneurs hire better people faster so they can focus on what matters most."

This statement shows our focus on entrepreneurs and our belief that better hiring allows business owners to better accomplish both their personal and professional goals.

Once you have a purpose statement, it's time to ask yourself, "Why?" Ask the same question about your own purpose—until you run out of answers.

Purpose statement:

Our company exists to help entrepreneurs hire better people faster so they can focus on what matters most.

Why is that important?

I care about helping entrepreneurs focus on the things that are truly important.

Why is that important?

I think a lot of entrepreneurs started out on a journey looking for something more, and they've lost sight of it. And I want to help them get back to that.

Why is that important?

I have personally been there. I get how hard it is to take time away from friends, family, and fun in order to focus on a business.

Why is that important?

If their business is successful, they'll be able to go back to their friends, family, and fun.

Why is that important?

I grew up with an entrepreneurial father who went through that same journey.

Why was that important?

As much as I have a great relationship with my dad, there were times when I didn't get to see him as a kid.

Why is that important?

I refuse to have that for myself or anyone else.

BINGO! See how personal that is? That type of personal answer resonates with people because you are sharing your deepest *why* with applicants and your team.

It's the honest, deep truth behind why Core Matters was founded. And that's why it's central to how the business runs.

When you hit your Core Purpose, it drives every decision, project, and issue in your company. This is the breath of life that your company needs to propel it toward everything you've ever wanted.

This was certainly the case for Reseco Insurance. Leaders in the company realized their Core Purpose was "Better Business. Better Lives." Every decision they make has to pass the question "How will this make better businesses or better lives?" If it can't pass that, it isn't aligned. They don't just quote insurance, they uncover the strategic goals of the company they are working for, and they implement strategies to make the business more secure. Often, these are counter to selling more premiums. This purpose allowed them to become a market leader in insurance and build a respected name as a partner in risk reduction.

Like Reseco, once your Core Purpose is defined, you have the perfect filter for all decisions going forward, including hiring.

CORE STORY

Your Core Values, Core Vision, and Core Purpose are not independent of one another. They are all part of the Core that makes up who you and your company are.

For that reason, you need a story that brings all these components together, so they resonate with the people you want to hire.

The Core Story will put your Core components together to answer four questions:

1. What is your company's *why*?

2. What problem does your company solve?

3. How do you solve the problem?

4. Why are you building a team?

If you can answer these questions and connect them to the rest of your Core through compelling language, you have a story that your future employees can tell themselves about your organization. It's a story the best will want to be a part of—and a story that will help you hire people you didn't think were out there.

Creating Your Core Story

To build your story, answer these four questions one at a time—while always keeping your Core Values, Core Vision, and Core Purpose in mind.

1. What is your company's why?

This is where your Core Purpose goes. Share your *why* in story form. Include the responses to the five whys and relate it back to your ideal employee.

As Simon Sinek says, you lead with *why* because that's what people care about most.

2. The problem your company solves

A good *why* must have a good *what* behind it. Here you must clearly communicate *what* your business solves related to that *why*.

To answer this, think about that connection: how does your *why* impact what you do? The problem you solve is never to fix air conditioners, improve air quality, or build something new. When people pay someone for a service or product, they do so because the service or product represents a practical yet deeper solution.

The same is true of your best employees. They buy into your company because it represents more than a paycheck to them—it represents a solution they believe in. If a new hire is only interested in making money, they aren't likely to last.

Think about it from the perspective of the client or customer. At the deepest level, customers don't want the window, the roof, or the new air conditioning unit. They want safety, peace of mind, or comfort. They want to avoid getting sick. They want their kids to be healthy.

Our clients want time for themselves, their families, and their friends. They want success that doesn't require them to give every moment to their company.

Dig as deeply as you can into this question. Many home service companies say they offer comfort. In the HVAC world, their salespeople are often called comfort consultants. But that isn't the final, deepest reason people pay for a new AC unit. They are paying to avoid a fight with their wife in the middle of the night about who gets the sheets. They are paying to relax and cool down after they get in from a run. They are paying for the ability to run around indoors with the kids without sweating.

Do you see how quickly that problem becomes a story?

So, the question to ask is: what is the *real* reason people are taking their hard-earned money and paying your company? And how does it tie into why you started this company in the first place?

3. How do you solve the problem?

You know there is no replica of your company. You've discovered why you do it. So now, how do you do things differently? Your uniqueness in solving your customer's problem is a huge point of attraction to certain workers. The right people want to be part of that very solution. So, it needs to be clear in your story.

We worked with two companies in the tree-trimming business. They do the same work, but one company's Core Story is about ease of service. They attract busy professionals that want a call-and-get-it-done type of experience.

On the other hand, the second company sees the yard as a sanctuary for you to relax in and their story shares how the tree is manicured. The way you present your yard is about your life and the dreams that you have for a safe haven.

One focuses its solution on efficiency. One focuses on the aesthetic value of the work. Each has a philosophy about their process. They both trim trees but have very different perspectives on the problem they solve and how they solve it.

And because of those different perspectives, they attract different workers. When workers apply, they know precisely what solution they are meant to implement, and they're already on board.

4. Why are you building a team to do this?

You need good people. You want to grow. You want to see your company quickly become bigger and better. And you want more time and energy to dedicate to your life.

But these aren't the only reasons you're building a team. It's time to find those reasons and share them with your current and potential future team members.

So, what is it about growing the business that excites you? Is it surrounding yourself with people smarter and more talented than you? Do you love seeing those around you thrive? Or do you just believe so intensely in serving your customers that you can't stand turning work away any longer?

The truth is, you have a deep reason why building a team matters, and that *why* fuels your desire to grow your team.

We recently had a client draft a team statement about their reasons for growing: "As our team grows, so does our expertise, market share, and authority in our industry. Building a large team of aligned employees, we're able to quickly improve the lives of those in our community."

Another client made it deeply personal: "As business owners, we believe it is our God-given purpose to serve our team by creating opportunities for them to grow. We will focus on building up our people so they can achieve so much more. By serving them well, we glorify God."

Your statement here doesn't have to be flashy (although it can be). And it definitely shouldn't speak to everyone. This is a chance to be authentic with people about why you're hiring them. That way, those who authentically connect with it will want to join your team, and those who don't will never apply.

This is the final piece of your story. It's the piece that speaks directly to your potential hires. It's why you need them, and why you will value them once they apply.

Bringing It All Together

These four questions come together to create your Core Story. With each piece in place, all you have to do is string it together and add a little personality and depth. For instance, this is a Core Story from Windy City Equipment:

> *We change the narrative. We set the standard for treating our customers better than they're used to. To be looked at as a partner in their business and align our objectives as one team to achieve results.*

> *We create a new level of transparency using modern technology. To open our customers' eyes to the skill and intelligence necessary to complete a repair by teaching instead of explaining.*

> *We tear down the wall that is in front of so many amazing people in HVACR and give those people an opportunity to succeed and grow in an industry that the world can't live without.*

> *We solve facilities managers' problems by putting relationships over transactions, quality over cost, communication over concealment, and honesty over everything else.*

> *We keep downtime to a minimum, prolong the life of equipment, and ensure proper operation, and at the root we're the partner they trust. Give their time back by doing it right the first time, keep them up to date on the information, and ensure they know the work performed and understand the price charged.*

> *When they pick up the phone to call us, it's an opportunity to strengthen the relationship.*

We are aligned, both with the customer and with one another. Understanding what we're doing and how everyone's work impacts the goal.

We endlessly improve every single day to ensure that we are ahead of the curve on technology, industry trends, and manufacturer training. We rely heavily on communication, largely through technology, to keep all departments and our customers informed every step of the way. And we encourage everyone in the company to take ownership of their duties and use the learning experiences as stepping stones for growth.

We are constantly streamlining our procedures. We equip our staff with the tools they need to perform the job in the most effective way possible. And we push each other to be better than we were yesterday so we can better take care of the customer.

With an ever-growing team we expand our reach, both geographically and demographically, and ultimately our success. It gives us the ability to unite over a common vision and collectively work toward it. Team members often work alone and are expected to get the job done quickly, efficiently, and correctly every single time. The bottom line is that the only way to win is to do it well and do it together.

We are the elite. And we prove it.

This story has attracted numerous great employees to work with them. It has the benefit of being completely true to their vision, values, purpose, and history. It's a true story, and it speaks to the type of people they want working with them. And as an added bonus, it brought in more great customers.

SHARE YOUR CORE

Now that you have defined your Core, it's time to share it online and in all your marketing materials. You can put it on your website, in YouTube videos, and around the office. You especially want to include it in your job postings.

You want to show the pride you and everyone at your company feels about your Core Values, Core Vision, Core Purpose, and Core Story. This is who you are, and these statements reflect who you want working for you.

Getting clear and authentic with who you really are and where you are going is the first step in permanently solving your hiring issues. Once this is in place, you can focus your attention on finding those people who respond to these words most.

TAKE ACTION

Go back to each section to do the work of how to figure out your Core Values, Core Vision, Core Purpose, and Core Story. Remember to involve your team.

Checklist

☐ Complete a Core Values brainstorming session and sort them into the correct category to narrow your values to three to five that are Core to you.

☐ Get clear on your Core Vision by figuring out where you want your company to be and how it will impact your team when you get there.

☐ Determine your Core Purpose by asking "why?" and clarifying what drives you to do what you do.

☐ Draft your Core Story by bringing your Core Values, Core Vision, and Core Purpose together in a narrative that attracts the right people and compels them to join your team.

☐ Update your marketing assets to include the components of your Core and build a process to make sure everyone on your team knows each one.

☐ Rewrite your job postings to incorporate the components of your Core so that they are compelling to the right people (more on job ad writing in the next chapter).

3

FIND

I was in the audience when Ryan was giving a workshop at Phoenix Sky Harbor Airport. In his talk, he mentioned the problem with most job descriptions. Because legal and compliance teams write them, Ryan mentioned that they become enormously long in order to cover everything those teams can imagine.

Every time a person gets fired, quits, or doesn't perform, someone pulls up the job description to see what it says. If rules weren't clearly stated, another bullet point gets added to the list.

Ryan said that in five years, those documents can reach five pages long. And at that point, nobody ever qualifies for the job again.

Hearing that, I knew I had something to show Ryan. After delivering the talk, my team approached him.

*"Remember that job description you were talking about?"
I asked. "We have one right here."*

*I slid over a packet of papers. It was a job description for
an electrician—a position we were currently hiring for.
As Ryan had said, it had grown over several years and
covered duties that electricians didn't even do.*

It was seven pages long.

—HARRIET, manager at Phoenix Sky Harbor Airport

If you remember from Ryan's story about fishing, the guide took
him right to the spot. Fishing can be relatively quick. All it takes
is putting the right bait into the right water for the particular
fish you want to catch. But that's the challenge, isn't it? If you
want to attract good people, you have to know where to find
good people and how to interest them in joining your company.

Most employers limit their fishing to job boards. They post ads
and hope they get results. But finding good hires this way is
extremely rare. According to CareerPlug, 82 percent of applicants come from job boards, while only 1.3 percent of them get
hired.

Essentially, they cast their line into the same lake as everyone
else, use the same bait, and hope they catch the prize fish. But if
you want the best prospects to bite, you need to change the way
you go about finding applicants.

THE LAW OF ATTRACTION

If you were looking to start a new personal relationship, how would you go about it? It can be an intimidating prospect, especially if you're out of practice. But almost all of us would ask some very big, important questions up front:

- What type of person am I looking to date?

- Where would I look for them?

- How would I attract them?

Most people know what they want from a new relationship. Some just want to meet someone new. Others are looking for that special person to start a family with. And if you were getting out there in the dating world, you'd have better luck if you knew precisely what you were looking for.

Having those preferences nailed down is no good, though, if you don't know where you're going to meet a new romantic partner. Are you going to use a dating app? Are you going to visit singles nights? Are you going to let your friends know you're on the market and let them set you up?

The best way to go about this is to think about *where* the type of person you're looking for is most likely to be looking for someone like you.

And then, once you meet that new person, you've got that last issue: how are you going to improve your chances that they are attracted to you?

You'd probably clean yourself up—get a haircut, buy some new cologne or perfume, buy new outfits that make you look good, and polish up your charming conversation skills.

But just as importantly, you'd make sure you brought out the qualities that you're looking for in others. If you want someone to go on adventures with around the globe, you'd talk to them about the time you went on a whirlwind tour of Italy and the scuba diving lessons you had in the Philippines last year. If you want someone who keeps up with your intellectual interests, you'd mention the books you've recently read or your favorite documentary.

Overall, you'd set out with someone particular in mind, go to the right places to find them, and create the circumstances where you could hit it off. That's your best shot at love.

It's also your best shot at hiring great employees. And just as you would start the dating process by thinking of the profile of your ideal partner, you have to start the finding process by creating a profile of your ideal employee—the Core Fit Profile.

THE CORE FIT PROFILE

Finding the right people requires you to know who the right people are. Instead of molding applicants into a position, you want those best suited for the work to show up at your door, eager to take the job.

To do that, you have to know what you're looking for. And that requires the Core Fit Profile.

This profile is the foundation of all messaging, placements, and tactics taken throughout the recruiting process, as it provides detailed information about "who" you'll be targeting. In the same way, you wouldn't spend money on marketing for new customers without determining who you're marketing to. You can't attract the right people until you know who those right people are.

For this reason, the Core Fit Profile is a game changer in how you recruit. It's a write-up that describes your ideal fit for a role. When you're done, you'll know who you need, how to craft a job ad that speaks to them, what you need to ask them in an interview, and how to measure their success.

To build the profile, you must fill in seven critical criteria:

1. Vision alignment

2. Core responsibilities

3. Measurable activities

4. Job description analysis

5. Disqualifying indicators

6. Behavioral requirements

7. Personal motivators

Each piece will bring us closer to those great hires, bringing clarity to who you need in each position in our organization.

Vision Alignment

At this point, you're clear on your Core, including the vision for where your company is headed and the values that hold your company together.

Now you need to create a way to ensure that any new hire fits your core values, vision, and purpose.

Vision alignment is about making sure the potential employee is committed to where you're going.

A lack of alignment can come from the noblest of places. We once worked with an electrical company where the owner was very passionate about helping underprivileged people and viewed the work as a ministry to create opportunity. The sales leader had an equally noble motivation. For him, the vision was to reduce energy consumption and save the planet.

The team struggled to gain traction and hire well because these two leaders were pulling in different directions.

One of our clients is an HVAC contractor who runs a business that is very unique in his space. The problem he solves has nothing to do with conditioning air, as it's much deeper than that. It's about health.

When he brought us in, he was close to giving up on the idea he'd ever find workers as passionate as him about his customer's health. There was a question he asked all his customers: how well does your home breathe? He explained to us that a home is like a person's body. If your home isn't breathing well, you're going to get sick.

He had a breakthrough moment when we were developing his vision. "If I want my team to reflect my passion," he told us, "I need to start looking for people who care about the things I care about."

He realized that his best workers came in feeling the way he did about HVAC. Many of them came from families who had little kids with asthma because of poor air quality. These workers were excited about helping families improve the health of these children.

The workers he hires now don't see themselves as HVAC techs. They're not customer service agents. They're champions of health for their customers. They empathize with what their customers are going through. They want to help people live healthier lives.

The same should be true for every position. A new sales representative should believe in the Core Values and Core Vision of the company. They'll sell more if they are aligned to your Core and believe in what they're selling. The more a team member is aligned to your Core, the more engaged and productive they'll be. And engaged, productive employees create happier customers and generate more profits.

Core Responsibilities

An employee who believes in your vision is important, but only if they can fulfill the core responsibilities of their position. To find the right candidates, then, you need clarity on those critical things you hire this person for. What are their Core Responsibilities?

For example, a sales rep may have many tasks they must do on a regular basis, but they should only have three to five Core Responsibilities. For one recent client of ours, those responsibilities were:

1. Qualified lead generation

2. Meet quota

3. Follow the sales process (including notes and follow-up)

That short, clear list allows you to focus on how well potential candidates measure up to the most important components of the job.

To generate your own list, ask yourself:

- What is essential for this role?

- What happens if these responsibilities aren't met?

In the case of that sales rep position, our client's company wouldn't be able to grow. They couldn't fulfill their vision. And sales reps would be more likely to miss their income goals and leave the company.

In other words, those responsibilities were essential, core components of the job.

How an employee fulfills those responsibilities should not be a major concern in the Core Fit Profile. Don't worry about how they complete these tasks here. The aim is simply to make sure an applicant sees these responsibilities as a priority and commits to always completing them.

Measurable Activities

Now it's time to attach these Core Responsibilities to your metrics that allow you to measure the performance of your next new hire. It may seem counterintuitive to create metrics for a position that isn't yet filled—but this component is critical to hiring better people faster. Employees want to know what's expected of them *before* they take a new job. Beyond that, thinking about the post-hire process makes a huge difference in how you think about every aspect of hiring.

In some companies, a metric is known as a scorecard or KPI. It's the number you use to assess the quality and productivity of a person's work.

To set successful measurements, they must fit four criteria:

1. They have to address a Core Responsibility directly.

2. They have to be objectively measurable.

3. They have to be reportable in real time.

4. The employee must have control over them.

The purpose of measurable activities is that they allow the employee to know how well they are achieving their Core Responsibilities. Your aim in creating measurements is to allow employees to know how close they are to hitting their goals. For that to happen, they have to provide clear and accurate information on performance during the period when the employee can do something about it.

For instance, a technician needs to know how far behind expectations they are on revenue generation or how they are performing with client expectations. If they don't know, they can't improve.

Many companies miss out on one or more of these key components of measurement. We once worked with a company that hired a new bookkeeper and set one of the scorecards to profitability. But profitability wasn't the bookkeeper's responsibility. Their responsibility was accurate financials. Imagine the frustration that bookkeeper felt when they were being held accountable for something they had no control over.

Other companies will make scorecards moving targets, adjusting expectations in the middle of a month or quarter for no apparent reason. This only discourages employees by denying them a win.

For metrics to be valuable, treat them like the scoreboard at a basketball game. The numbers are objective. They relate directly to performance on the court. And they remain in place until the final buzzer. That's how the players know how they're doing and how hard they must work.

We will come back to these measurables throughout the Core Fit Hiring System.

Job Description Analysis

It's time to analyze or create a job description for the position you're hiring. This is a legal document and different from a job ad, which we will get to later. A job description is a compliance document that HR or your legal team uses to hold people accountable. It's what they use to make decisions about whether or not workers keep their job.

Core Responsibilities should be in the job description. Measurable activities are there, too. Any physical requirements to do the job, like "Must be able to climb to certain heights," should be in there. All of this compliance stuff goes in a job description.

To complete this document, you want to get beyond the Core Responsibilities. Ask yourself what things they must do that aren't related to their core responsibilities. What activities need to be completed on a regular basis in this role? What functions must they do once or twice a year? What issues should they handle when they come up, such as refunds or customer complaints?

The aim is for the candidate to have a complete understanding of the role. You don't want to blindside them with expectations they didn't know you had.

For that reason, you want to keep this relatively short and to the point.

Avoid any and every possible requirement. Don't throw in a task because someone at one time or another didn't complete it. You want the candidate to know what you expect and how they can succeed in the role. Make that as clear as possible and as concise as you can.

Here's an example of how you can do this analysis.

The job description defines the following for the perfect candidate:

- Description of the functions of the job

- Definition of the needed skills to be successful on the job

- Detail of the experience required, if any, to do quality work

- Attitudes necessary

- How they think

- Their habits as they relate to the job functions

- Disqualifying indicators for each function

- Measurable activities to track their performance

- Minimum and expected measurements for each job functions

- Qualifying behaviors to test during the interview process

- Interviewing activity to test alignment with job function

For the following questions, think about a typical week for the job in question.

- What activities need to be completed on a regular basis? (list as many as you can)

- What activities, people, or systems are they responsible for on a regular basis?

- What other things must they do that aren't related to their core responsibilities?

- What functions of their job must they do once or twice a year? (project work)

- What activities will they deal with as they come up? (for example, customer complaints)

Describe a difficult situation they must be able to handle and how they will handle it.

It's also important to note that states have different laws in regard to job descriptions, so make sure yours are in line with local standards.

Disqualifying Indicators

Disqualifying indicators are the behaviors that you see as part of the interview process. Start by calling out disqualifying indicators in your Core Fit Profile. This allows you to be aware of them ahead of time so you can pick up on them and address these concerns right away. Think of these as "red flags."

Here, you are looking for traits that disqualify the candidate from the position.

For example, we personally screen for victim mentality. During a conversation, we're not explicitly asking a person if they're a victim. But if their responses show they tend to blame others, we address it before moving on. If they can't let go of it, they're out.

To find your disqualifying indicators, ask yourself what answers would suggest the person doesn't fit the responsibilities, values, and vision you have at your company.

If they don't have your Core Values, how would that show up in an interview? How do you test for someone with the wrong behavior patterns or who doesn't want to be part of your team?

You can start by looking at those Core Responsibilities again. For a sales rep position with a responsibility to generate leads, you could ask how they think leads should be generated. Do they feel as a salesperson that they have a responsibility to generate their own leads? If they don't, they aren't a good fit for the role.

Are they someone who believes in following the process or will they give up after the first call if they don't get a response?

Once you know what is disqualifying, you can build interviews around those points. This will help you avoid hiring someone who doesn't fit with your company's culture or the role. And you avoid wasting everyone's time.

Behavioral Requirements

When we ask business leaders to describe a "good employee," they rarely describe the work they do. They often start with things like "they show up on time, they follow the rules, or they speak up when there is a problem."

In other words, they look at the employee's behavior.

To find the right people for your company, you must figure out what characteristics or behaviors your ideal person needs to have.

To ensure you're bringing in people with the right attitudes, management style, and communication strategies, you need to build a Core Fit Profile with the ideal traits and behaviors for the role. Once you have this, you have something to compare against so you know if the applicant matches or not.

To build a Core Fit Profile, you'll need to rely on a prehire assessment. If you aren't using prehire assessments in your recruiting today, the minimal investment will save you a fortune down the road.

These surveys report on a person's behavior and they all have a different approach to creating their reports. They can help you quickly determine if the person is right for the role.

They are great for avoiding role–person mismatches, bad culture fits, and conflicts later on. When you use them you aren't looking for a replica of you. You use them to consider the traits you need in other people to round out the team.

Personal Motivators

Some prehire assessments will help you to determine what motivates potential hires. Personal motivation is key in good hiring. When you're building out your Core Fit Profile, you should ask yourself, "How would the right person in this role be motivated?" and "Can I provide stimulus for this motivation?"

As an example, when hiring a sales rep, you might want them motivated by making more money. But you also want them motivated by winning and closing the sale. Money may be the obvious motivator here, but that desire to win is what really makes a great salesperson.

If someone lacks the right motivations or is motivated by something you cannot provide, it's best to figure that out *before* you hire them.

One of our clients does civil construction work with very tight deadlines. Schedule flexibility is something they can't offer. After completing their Core Fit Profile, they had determined that the right type of worker for them is someone who likes a structured schedule with deadlines. Unfortunately, they had hired some people who were fighting for more flexibility. Understanding motivators alone would have saved them the headache of hiring the wrong people.

The aim here is to find the right motivational fit for your industry, values, and vision. Getting your team to be engaged and productive is much easier with the right motivators in place.

Creating the Core Fit Profile

To put all this information together into a Core Fit Profile might take some time, but the value is immense. Once you have a Core Fit Profile, writing a job ad or developing interview questions takes only a matter of minutes. You'll end up targeting the right type of employee for your company and the position.

You'll want to develop a Core Fit Profile for every position at your company as each one is different. Don't worry, once you have the first one done, it's much easier to create the rest.

You will use the Core Fit profile for many of the things you'll learn in the rest of the book, including:

- Writing the job ad

- Developing the interview questions

- Figuring out where to advertise the job

In other words, it's essential.

WRITING THE JOB AD

There are entire books written on writing job ads, but you can transform the impact of your ads through one key mindset shift. Instead of taking the job description that HR gives you and simply posting it online, you should take that job description, plug it into the Core Fit Profile, and use it to create a story that gets people excited to apply for the job.

As we've already discussed, a job description is a compliance-related HR document that you are legally required to provide an applicant. A job description rarely motivates anyone to apply to a position. If you want applicants excited, you have to transform the dry, complex job description into an ad for your company, your team, and the job.

Think about how car companies sell cars. When Chevy releases a new Corvette, they don't focus on the details about the high price or the expensive maintenance required. Those details are always available; instead, the advertisement focuses on the fun and the adventure of driving a fast, beautiful machine.

They show young, happy people driving with the top down on a coastal highway or a businessman in an expensive suit flying down a glamorous city street before going to a movie premiere.

They make commercials like that because people buy things that they think they will enjoy or that will make them happy or fulfilled. And when you post a job ad on a job board or on your website, you are asking someone to buy into your Core and how this job will help them personally.

For example, if a skilled tech is looking for a job, they know what a skilled tech does. They don't want to read an ad about what is expected. They want to read about an exciting workplace, meaningful work, an incredible team, and how much fun they'll have being a part of it.

In other words, they want to read what is in it for them if they get this job.

That's the purpose of your job ad. Like advertising a new car, you want it to stand out and to make the case why this is a great position anyone with the right skills and right attitude will love.

At the same time, just like that car ad, you want to make sure to repel the wrong type of applicant. Chevy doesn't want a bunch of people coming in to test drive their Corvettes who can't afford one or who have different needs in a vehicle. Nor do they want a bunch of their Corvette customers coming in to buy a Trailblazer instead.

For that reason, the ads show precisely what each vehicle has to offer. The Corvette commercial shows the top down, the high speed, and the luxury, while the Trailblazer commercial shows a family and the extra space for packing bags and going on a road trip.

That way, everyone knows right away which car is for them—and which one isn't.

So, how do you make your job ad speak to your ideal hires and get them excited to work for you?

For starters, your job ad needs to include your core story. It's what sets you apart. It's what makes you different. When a potential applicant reads your story, they'll know your vision, your values, your purpose. They'll know if they want to be a part of your culture and your team. And that story will have much more impact than a bulleted list of responsibilities.

You also have to show that you have a track record for rewarding success. Make it clear what you expect by laying out what good performance looks like and how good performance is rewarded.

Of course, an ad only matters if people know what you're advertising. That's why Chevy always puts the name of the car in big letters. For a job ad, that means using job titles that everyone understands.

We often see employers who want to stand out by coming up with job titles that are simply too clever for their own good.

Job seekers just scroll past those posts because they don't know what they mean.

We've seen "chief chatter" used to describe a call center manager position, "catalyst" for an office manager, and even "retail Jedi" for a shop assistant—but every time these titles did more harm than good.

We had a client who had been running an ad for three months and had only received two applications—both from low-quality applicants.

When we asked what the job title was, they told us, "Panel Technician." When we reviewed the ad, though, the job was clearly for general laborer. In other words, they needed unskilled applicants, but the job title suggested it was a specialist position.

"Just for fun," we said, "let's change the title to general laborer and repost it."

Within four days, the company had 105 applications from qualified candidates.

With these ideas in mind, you have the basic pieces for assembling a job ad. As you put your ad together, use a template that involves six sections:

- **Job Title**—Make it clear what this job actually is so the right people see it and the job boards categorize it correctly.

- **The Lead-In**—This is a quick two- or three-sentence hook that gets the applicant's attention.

- **Company Overview**—This is where you put your core story.

- **"What's in It for Me?"**—Here, you tell them why they should care and why they should be excited to work for you in this position.

- **The Three "Rs"**—This is really three separate sections that cover requirements, rewards, and responsibilities. This is the stuff that you pull from your typical job description but sell in a way that top performers will take notice.

- **Call to Action**—Tell the potential applicant what they should do next.

With these six sections, you give an applicant everything they need to know about your company and the job. By the end, they'll be excited to apply, and they'll know if they'd be a good fit for the work.

As you craft your job ad, aim for the appropriate length—ours tend to be on the longer side. It's true that shorter job ads might bring in more applications, but longer ads produce higher-quality applicants.

Longer ads discourage those who are applying en masse for whatever position they can get. That length also shows that your company is serious about hiring someone who is a fit. It gives you the space to describe your culture and really describe what is exciting about this position.

Your ad should be at least six hundred words—that's almost three times the standard job ad. We've had some that are more than two thousand words, and they got amazing results!

As you put the finishing touches on your ad, there's one final piece you need to include: the pay. Companies go back and forth on whether to include salary, but we've found that job ads that include pay perform significantly better. In fact, research has found that 91 percent of applicants want a salary range in a job listing. When you give them what they want, they'll be more likely to apply.

Posting the salary also shows that you're transparent and ensures anyone applying is comfortable working for what you're offering. It puts an end to the salary negotiation games that we're all familiar with. List the range you're willing to pay and let the applicant decide.

360 MARKETING PLAN

Now that you have a Core Fit Profile and your job ad, you need to get the word out. And to do that, we need to talk about marketing.

This is often the point at which clients do a double take. Marketing? For hiring?

That's exactly right.

**Recruiting is a marketing activity,
and everyone is responsible for it.**

The value of this mindset is twofold. In the first place, it means you should be investing in marketing to your potential hires the same way you market to customers. You should be looking to place information about positions in the spaces your best potential hires are. Second, everyone connected to your organization has a role to play in bringing the best quality applicants to your door.

To understand the role everyone has to play, you need to do a 360 Marketing Plan for your entire organization.

The 360 Marketing Plan gives you a look at every single angle of your business and all the help you can get with recruiting. It shows all the ways you can engage your employees, your vendors, your customers, and other resources in the community to create a robust and effective way to get more qualified applicants.

Your employees are a walking, talking billboard for your company. Your team wants to see you hire great people. If everyone believes in your Core, they must believe in recruiting the best people. These people will help you achieve your vision and demonstrate your values.

THE 360 MARKETING PLAN

All you have to do is equip them with the tools to promote your brand to their friends and family.

The same is true of your external customers. We talk to business owners all the time who are convinced they can't let their customers know they're hiring. They protest, "Our customers might think we can't serve them!"

But this doesn't make any sense. Your customers come to your company because they know you'll deliver. And if they're your loyal customers, they're also some of the best candidates and ambassadors for your growing team. Customers have family and friends who need good jobs where there's a sense of purpose. This opportunity for them to recruit for you can only exist if you share your job ads with them.

Shamrock Solutions is a managed services provider, and they suddenly realized the magnitude of this in one of our coaching sessions. During the session, the sales leader posted a message on LinkedIn aligned to their Core Fit Profile. Until now, he'd avoided posting on his LinkedIn because it was filled with customer prospects, customers, and referral partners. Within two hours of posting, he had six messages for six different possible candidates for a position they had been struggling to fill for over eight months.

A 360 Marketing Plan identifies how to get everyone around you recruiting organically so you grow your team with the right people.

The 360 Marketing Plan will help you answer these questions:

- What marketing channels exist for your recruiting efforts?

- How do you market and promote through these channels?

- How do you equip your team to help you recruit?

- How do you market externally to your ideal employees?

- How do you market to your partners so they can help you with recruiting?

- How do you market to your customers in a way that engages their support?

Here are some examples to get your creative juices flowing. And don't stop with these ideas. You should work with your marketing team to develop the best word-of-mouth recruiting systems to get people talking the most.

Current Employees

Your team doesn't think about recruiting nearly as often as you do, so think about the tools and the training you can provide to get them recruiting for you.

People who love where they work are likely to share the experience, but only if you ask them to. Imagine your best people posting videos and photos about their workplace experience. Now their friends want to work for you too, and they are more likely to stay. According to Gallup, employees with a best friend at work are seven times more likely to be engaged in their job.

Industry Partners

Share your stories about company events when talking with industry partners. Celebrate with them and don't hold back. When you make an effort to share, you create an aura around you. Everyone soon understands how awesome it is to work for you.

Local Communities

Alternatively, you could take the sponsorship deal you have for the local Little League team and use that space for marketing your jobs. One of the parents of those kids may be looking for a new and better opportunity.

Industry Competitors

You can get very creative with these efforts. We once had a client who asked one of his competitors for recruitment support. The competitor was wrapping up several jobs at once and was facing the possibility of laying off some of his team. Our client asked if he could borrow employees, pay a three-dollar-an-hour premium to offset any risk the competitor was taking, and use them to crank out some work. This kept the team employed and working and allowed him to take on more jobs. Everybody won, and his stress went away instantly.

With a 360 Marketing Plan, you expand your options to reach those better hires. You don't just market yourself online to job boards and social media, you can build a network around your biggest fans—the people who are most invested in seeing you succeed.

The beauty of a 360 Marketing Plan is you can get in front of job seekers before they're even looking.

That's why the 360 Marketing Plan is so powerful. It's redirecting your marketing efforts toward your greatest need: recruiting. You still get all the other benefits of traditional campaigns, but now all your stakeholders will be recruiting for you too.

If you expand your search efforts to focus on your Core Fit Profile and a 360 Marketing Plan, all of the sudden, you won't be fishing with a single line in a random lake, you'll be casting nets in every body of water in the area. And you'll know immediately when you have the right catch.

360 MARKETING PLAN OUTLINE

With this shift in mindset, you can work with your marketing team to outline a concrete 360 Marketing Plan. The strategies you develop will be, by their very nature, unique to your business, but there are certain tactics that work across many companies and industries. Here are a few to get you started.

Improve Internal Communications

Far too often, companies stop sharing their Core at the leadership level. If you want your team to be ambassadors to the community, you need to make sure they understand your Core as well as you do.

Build up internal communications and find internal champions who can share these ideas across your organization.

Most importantly, make sure hiring information is getting to those who could recommend the company to others. We often ask employees at new clients how many people their company is hiring. The response? The employees didn't even know the company was hiring in the first place.

We've had people tell us that they thought their boss didn't care that there weren't enough workers to get jobs done. It's not always obvious to your people that you're working on the problem, so you have to remind them—a lot!

Your people need to know what positions you're hiring for and what the Core Fit Profile is for an ideal candidate. Only then can they help you find the right people for the job.

Communicate the Employee Experience

What are your employees and other stakeholders going to tell the best potential hires about your business? You want them to show just how great your company is. To do that, you need to equip them to demonstrate that fact.

You need employee testimonials, videos that show a day in the life at the company, and articles that can chart a potential career path. You need content that shows why your company is better than all the competition in all those areas.

That is what makes the difference to those future applicants.

Create Consistent Marketing Materials

Before you go sharing everything externally, take a moment to review all your marketing materials and make sure everything is aligned. We often work with clients who have hired multiple marketing organizations over the years, and their marketing materials are all over the place. They have multiple logos, use different fonts, and have vastly different words to describe the company.

This clutter works against you because no one can fully grasp who your company is, and the really valuable information gets lost. So, your aim has to be to get back to basics. Focus on that Core until it's dialed in and in front of everyone.

Share Your Message Externally

You have a website, and very likely, your company has some social media presence. You may also sponsor events. It's time to share the internal language you've developed for your Core through those external channels.

Update your website with the new Core Values, Core Vision, Core Purpose, and Core Story. Pin your Core Vision to the top of your social media pages.

And get used to sharing new content around your company's identity with those interested in your company.

You should use every outlet available. If there are job boards that allow free postings, use those. Take your testimonials and put them on YouTube. Then share across platforms. Make sure everywhere you look online, your brand and your message is attractive to the right type of person you are looking to hire.

Retool Your Marketing

It's time to start advertising directly to potential hires. You likely already run ads on social media and Google. Why not take a small part of that advertisement budget and focus it on recruiting? We've discovered that ads targeted to recruiting will do an equally good job of attracting customers, while the inverse isn't true.

You already use SEO for blog posts for customers. Why not start writing SEO posts that speak to those looking for work? This is a relatively small expense that can get your company in front of the right people.

Choose and Get to Work

We've only touched the surface of the 360 Marketing Plan. This is far from an exhaustive list of potential strategies. The best improvement you can make is to get started on some part of this immediately. Your aim should be to pick the areas you can improve upon most and get to work on them right away.

TAKE ACTION

We won't lie. The Core Fit Profile and 360 Marketing Plan undeniably require some work. These are items you cannot create when you have a few minutes between tasks. They require research, deep thought, resources, and time.

But they're also great at helping you attract the best people to your company—people who believe in your Core and who are willing to do what it takes to help the company grow and succeed.

As Benjamin Franklin is credited with saying, "If you fail to plan, plan to fail."

And failure, in this case, is continuing with the status quo.

So, build a Core Fit Profile for every position. Start with roles you are actively filling. Once you know what you're looking for, you can reach your best candidates through a 360 Marketing Plan that brings together all those who most want your company to succeed. Use your employees, your customers, your vendors and strategic partners. In some instances, you can even use your competitors.

Work with your marketing team to target each one of these stakeholders and equip them with the knowledge and tools to reach out to those they know would be a good fit for your company.

In every huge success story you read about in business, the leader always credits their team. Go make this your success story and build the incredible team you've always wanted.

Checklist

- ☐ Write a Core Fit Profile for every position in your company. Start with roles you're actively seeking to fill. Go back to the seven criteria in this chapter.

- ☐ Involve current employees in recruiting. Equip them with the information and the tools they need, like referral cards, social media posts, and even how to tell your Core Story.

- ☐ Retool your current marketing systems to regularly communicate open positions to your customers. If you have a customer newsletter, that's a great place to start.

- ☐ While networking and building relationships with industry partners, share your Core Story and equip partners with the information they need to recruit for you.

4

AUTOMATE

We run a company that checks inventory for large grocery stores like Kroger and Walmart. When we came to Ryan, we thought we had a fairly well-run hiring process. It didn't always net the best results, and was tedious and slow, but it seemed to run as efficiently as we could hope.

The first thing Ryan did was completely upset that assumption. He did it with a single sentence. He riffed on Isadore Sharp's famous line—"Systemize the predictable, so you can humanize the exceptional"—and said, "Smart business owners automate the predictable so they can focus on the important."

We'd never thought of automation that way. For us, automation was something you'd expect in factories or CRM software. It never occurred to us that it could work in the hiring process.

Yet, after just three weeks using even limited automation, we saw incredible results. We were able to completely eliminate our costs for sponsoring ads, and we saved our HR team twenty hours a week by removing the manual screening.

It saved us money, and it saved us time. Automation gave us the space to invest in the difference makers. And before long, it was making a difference.

—ADAM, Advanced Inventory Solutions

With all the value that comes from developing your Core and reaching the best applicants, the one objection we hear most from clients at this point is: who has time for all this?

If you're like most business owners, you probably wear twenty-seven different hats. A lot of those hats can be really enjoyable to wear—like getting your hands dirty working with your team, coming up with big new ideas for the company, or meeting interesting customers and providing a valuable service.

Recruiting is likely a hat you don't enjoy wearing, though—one you only wear because you *have* to wear it. It feels like a distraction—a responsibility that takes you away from what you do best in your business.

Wearing that hat often means it feels like you don't have time to develop a Core Fit Profile or build a 360 Marketing Plan.

It takes so much time and effort to keep the current system running that there's no time left to build a new one.

But what if you didn't have to wear that hat anymore? What if you could automate many of the hiring tasks that take up so much of your time?

You have likely seen automation's value in other areas of your company. For example, you may have a customer relationship management (CRM) system that automates much of your customer communication. This same value can be found in automation for the hiring process.

There are three components to automate recruiting:

1. **Technology**

2. **Delegation**

3. **Process**

Let's look at each component at a high level, so you can adopt automation to create a consistent, repeatable process for attracting the right people without taking up all your time.

TECHNOLOGY

There are many ways you can leverage technology to help you automate recruiting. The Applicant Tracking System (ATS) is perhaps the most powerful and effective. This is a system for managing most of your recruiting process. Like a CRM system that allows you to manage your customers through your marketing and sales process, an ATS allows you to streamline communication and manage your applicants through your recruiting and hiring process.

Even if you already have an ATS, there's much you can learn here about its potential and finding an ATS that serves all your needs. Clients often switch to a new ATS once they know what's possible with the right system. So, we recommend everyone read what's ahead.

An ATS provides you with a system to manage your applicants through a data-rich, repeatable process. Many of the steps you and your team spend hours on, a computer can easily complete for you. This frees up time and money and creates the opportunity to make better decisions across your company. An ATS helps you manage all of your job posts, keep track of applicants, collaborate with your team about potential hires, and automate communication with candidates. In short, it sets you free to focus on the important things while the ATS takes care of the predictable.

It does this while increasing applicant flow without spending more money on job board advertising. Most of our clients see the time savings alone as justification for the additional software expense. This was certainly the case at Advanced Inventory Solutions (AIS), where it only took three weeks to cut advertising spend and save twenty hours a week.

AIS wasn't an outlier, either. We see it day in and day out working with clients. According to a report from Talentlyft.com, 78 percent of recruiters who use an ATS say they see an improvement in the quality of the candidates they hire. Ninety-four percent of recruiters surveyed by Capterra.com say software has improved their hiring process.

One of our clients went from virtually no applicants to over 190 in four days. Now imagine if you also had the technology to sort through your applications, so you only ever saw the best candidates—right when they arrived at your office ready to be hired.

That's the potential of a quality ATS.

Choosing an ATS

There are hundreds, if not thousands, of applicant tracking systems out there, and we're often asked which one is the best. Our answer is always the same: "The one your team uses." Just like any tool in your business, if your ATS sits idle, there's no chance of it generating a return.

To find a platform that excites you and your team, there are some things you need to think through. After all, no ATS is perfect. Each offers trade-offs—strengths in some areas and limitations in others. To find the best ATS for you, you have to find the product that fits your specific needs.

There are six criteria to consider as you narrow your list:

1. Applicant Attraction

2. Integration

3. Reporting Capabilities

4. Communication

5. Implementation

6. Price

Each of these criteria is by their nature subjective. There's no single right answer, other than the right one for you and your team. For that reason, we will give you a list of questions to ask during your demo with the ATS company.

Your aim should be to find an ATS product that you can answer "yes" to as many of these questions across all six criteria as possible. That's the product that's right for your company.

Even if you already have an ATS, these criteria can help you grade its ability to perform for you—or your need to find a substitute.

Applicant Attraction

Fundamentally, if your ATS doesn't help you attract high-quality applicants, then it's not doing its job. Some are better than others when it comes to their ability to help you attract the right people to your team.

Here are a few questions you can ask your ATS sales rep to determine the system's capability to bring in better hires:

- Does the ATS have a clear and simple job search? If we have a lot of jobs open, can applicants come in and search through all our jobs easily?

- Does the ATS make it very simple for people to apply?

- Does the ATS make it easy to share our jobs on social media and with our employees?

- Does the ATS integrate with the most popular job boards for the industry that we're in?

For this last question, be specific about any industry-specific job boards you want to be a part of.

Your ATS won't be effective if it's too difficult for people to use or if the process of applying for one of your jobs is too lengthy. You have to find a balance between the applicant experience and the work your team has to do in processing the application.

Understanding how effective the ATS is at creating a great experience for the applicant will make sure you get a steady stream of applications.

Integration

Some systems are easier to set up and use than others. Ideally, you want an ATS that can integrate relatively easily with the systems you already have in place, allowing you to maximize the new product's value with minimal headaches.

Here are the questions to ask to determine if a particular ATS offers the integrations you need:

- Does the ATS have its own careers page? Is there a way to integrate it with our website?

- Do we have an HRIS that needs to be integrated? If so, does the ATS allow for this integration? (If someone in HR doesn't know, you likely don't have one and can skip this point.)

- Does the system have interview scheduling that integrates with our work calendar? (This is important if you want candidates to automatically schedule interviews with you, which is a real time-saver).

- Do we use prehire assessments? If so, does the ATS integrate with our prehire assessment platform?

- Is the system capable of importing candidates from another system?

If your team is already using software to support your people processes, it's worth the effort to explore integrating your ATS with those systems. Sometimes, you'll find a sleek ATS, but it won't integrate with your existing systems or processes—which will only slow your team down. It can also lead to mistakes in processing applications or onboarding new employees because the data has to be manually transferred.

Reporting

We'll review reporting when we get to Assess in Chapter 8.

In the meantime, it's important to know what the ATS can do when it comes to reporting so you can determine if it meets your needs.

- Does the ATS track our job board advertising spend?

- Does the ATS allow us to build custom recruiting and hiring reports?

- Does it allow us to generate EEO reports? Will we need them in the future?

- Do we need to determine the source (job boards, social, referral, etc.) of the application? (We recommend that you do, but not everyone needs this).

- Do we need data exports, and is the information usable?

The best recruiting processes are driven by data. It's why we've included the Assess component in the Core Fit Hiring System—more on that later. Better data equals better results and a greater speed at which to make adjustments so you can keep up with the market.

Communication

Communicating with applicants can be very time consuming, and we've already seen how the best applicants can be lost when a response doesn't come quickly enough. By letting the ATS do this for you, you can be certain you respond quickly and maintain interest, all while you are able to focus on the things that only you can do—like spend time with those interested in joining your team.

- Does the ATS send automated text messages and emails to applicants?

- Does it have built-in video interviewing capabilities or integrate with a third party?

- Does it allow us to send bulk emails to past candidates?

- Are we able to audit, track, and evaluate all job seeker communications?

- Does it include a full audit trail where we know every person on our team who logs in and updates the system? (This may be a compliance requirement in your industry).

- Does it log if a hiring manager has reviewed an application? What about notes from the interview?

- Does it allow us to send one-off communications to select candidates?

- Will it help us with the reference check process and email references on our behalf?

- Are we able to log the results of our background check to the candidate profile?

- If sending offer letters is important to us, does the ATS allow this? Does it have digital signature capability?

Remember, not all of these things may be important to your recruiting process. These questions are simply the most frequently asked when we're implementing an ATS for someone.

Implementation

Between setting up the system and training your team, rolling out an ATS can be just as challenging as choosing the product in the first place. If you don't have a team dedicated to the success of the rollout, it's bound to fail. Make sure you're working with an ATS provider that is able to support you every step of the way.

- Do they offer implementation support? Do they have an online knowledge base so you can self-service problems when they come up?

- Are you able to speak with a person when you need support?

- Are there special data requirements that your system has to maintain? Will the ATS provider help monitor those requirements?

- If you need to hire for multiple locations (offices, job sites, etc.), can you, or does it require you to have multiple instances of the platform?

Price Point

Applicant tracking systems range from nearly free to thousands of dollars per month. Find a system that meets your goals and won't break the bank. Also, with an ATS, more expensive does not necessarily mean better.

Many of those expensive products cost so much because of the expensive custom integration and enterprise features they offer.

Ultimately, there are only two questions you need to ask yourself when considering pricing:

- Is the price justified given our current hiring goals?

- Am I comfortable with the pricing structure and confident we can achieve a positive return on our investment?

Putting Your ATS to Use

At this point, you've taken the major step in selecting the ATS that is right for your company. Simply finding a product that your team will use is a big step toward hiring better people faster.

With your ATS ready, you can take the job ads you wrote when developing your Core Fit Profile and upload them exactly how you wrote them.

Turning on the automation in your ATS is often the hardest part for entrepreneurs. Everything about the ATS sounds great until you have to let a computer take on important responsibilities. Leaving screening up to a computer just feels risky. What if the perfect candidate slips through your fingers because a computer couldn't recognize what you were looking for? What if a computer serves up all the generic, mediocre applicants because they happen to tick the right boxes? What if an error in the code means the wrong email goes to the best person for the job?

We know it's a scary proposition to trust technology to take over this huge responsibility. But there's a way to do it that protects a company against those risks.

In business, you automate the predictable—the things that need to be done every time so the business won't fail—because those processes allow you to do those things right, every time. The automation of an ATS is no different. It's a tool that, when you build it up properly, will deliver on those important tasks, every time.

Turning On the Automation

With the job ad posted, you can start automating those important tasks of communicating with the applicant. This begins with setting up your ATS to automatically send applicants a text message or email when you receive an application.

So often, companies take days to send this first message—because it has to be sent by a real person who is doing a hundred other things. Those first few minutes are crucial. Respond too late and your best applicants may be gone.

Your new ATS changes that. Once they apply, your ATS can let them know you received their information within minutes. A standard response might look like this:

Thank you for applying for [ROLE].
We're looking forward to learning more about you.
We'll be in touch within 24 hours.

That commitment to a time frame for responding is crucial. You need to treat these incoming applications like you would a new customer lead. Set proper expectations for your response time and then follow through.

Your ATS can automatically send messages throughout the process. After you approve an application, it could automatically send a message that reads something like:

We received your application, and we'd like to schedule an [interview/phone call]. Please click this link to schedule.

At the same time, your ATS can send you a message that a new applicant matches the qualifications you need. That will allow you to send a personalized message that shows you are engaged in the hiring process and to make that first real connection with a potential new hire.

Those who don't match the qualifications should get a notification, too:

Thank you for applying, but at this time, we are pursuing candidates that more closely match the qualifications. We will keep you on our list and let you know of future opportunities unless you tell us otherwise.

The list of applicants that don't match perfectly will prove important, as we'll discuss shortly.

Successful applicants pick an interview time of their choosing. Once it's confirmed, the ATS sends another message that says:

I'm looking forward to meeting you on [DATE]. By the way, punctuality is critical to your success here, so make sure you're at least five minutes early to the interview.

With these automations in place, the interview will be the first time you spend any meaningful time on that candidate's application.

Best of all, this entire process can happen within a few hours. At this speed, a great applicant is engaged and booked.

By automating these tasks, you discover the best applicants and start engaging the applicant right away without requiring any time on your part. The time you used to spend poring over applications (or paying someone in HR to do so) is now freed up for more essential work—or for you to finally take a break and enjoy life a bit.

That's the real promise of quality automation.

DELEGATION

You can also use automation technology to improve hiring results and reduce the hours spent on applications by delegating some of the responsibility for qualifying for a position to the people applying. By asking the right screening questions, you can get the wrong applicants to knock themselves out of the running for a position without lifting a finger yourself.

You do this through knockout questions.

Knockout questions are those you ask applicants to complete when they submit their application. To come up with your knockout questions, think about the nonnegotiables. Stick to no more than five questions—three is better. You don't need to know so much you can make a hire, just enough to know if you want to talk to them.

Here are some questions you could consider:

- Are you authorized to work in this country? (Y/N)

- Are you able to perform the physical components of the job? (Y/N)

- Do you have XXX certification? (Y/N)

- Why do you want to join our team? (open-ended)

We'll dig more into screening questions during the next chapter on interviews. For now, focus on absolute deal-breakers. Keep in mind you may not need some of these, especially if you're not receiving applications that would get knocked out. For example, we rarely ask the applicant if they're over eighteen. The number of applicants we get that are under eighteen is minimal and not worth using one of the knockout questions.

Your ATS can then score each applicant's answers and filter out the applicants who don't pass. It can review qualifications and remove those applicants who don't fit before anyone has to take a second to look at an application.

Don't worry. The ATS doesn't decide how aggressive this screening process is. That's entirely up to you. If applications seem easy to get and you have a lot coming in, be more aggressive. In a tougher market for the position, recalibrate to let more applicants through to the next stage.

Ideally, every knockout question is multiple choice. Multiple-choice questions can help your ATS move applications forward for you. Open-ended questions make the application process harder for you and the job seeker. This is the first interaction with your company for most job seekers, and creating roadblocks this early in the stage can discourage them. They may choose not to complete your application at all. And you will have more to sort through, and actually read, if you use open-ended questions.

That's not a reason to eliminate open-ended questions entirely. You want to at least ask a final question that will help you screen: "Why do you want to join our team?" We've had applicants answer that with, *I need the money, I need a job,* or *My last boss fired me.* Answers to this question are very telling about how an applicant thinks about this job and their future with your company.

These aren't always disqualifiers. Sometimes, the answers you get immediately show a values match. If they share something extremely relevant to your company and your vision, you know you are on the right track for a long-lasting employee. One construction company we worked with was obsessed with new technology. They wanted to hire people who get excited about new technology too. So when an applicant wrote, "I want to work with a cutting-edge company," the managers got excited. There was clear value and vision alignment. And that answer caught their eye precisely because it was the only answer they actually had to look at.

If you need further screening before the interview, you can automate more qualifying steps that further put the responsibility on the job seeker to qualify themself.

We set up one painting company to go from application to scheduled interview within three hours. The ATS reviewed all the closed-ended questions, and the open-ended questions were saved for the interview. The owner didn't even touch the application until the applicant walked in the door. The system did all the work.

Once an applicant answered the prescreen questions above correctly, the system sent them this text message:

Hey, we really like you! We've got a couple more questions. Click this link to get started.

Then the applicant was asked three more multiple-choice questions that went a little bit deeper on skills and experience. The system graded those, too. Once it did, the system sent that link to the calendar for an interview or the rejection response.

When the owner looked at the application, they had a qualified, eager applicant sitting in front of them, ready for an interview.

Advanced Screening

The above ATS automation tools are lifesavers for busy, overworked entrepreneurs looking for the next great hire. They're even great for busy, overworked HR teams. But there's even more you can do to improve the screening process and bring the best candidates to the interview.

Employers often complain that job seekers don't read the job ad before they apply—and our research would support this. Knowing this, though, we can use that fact to our advantage to screen out careless applicants and secure a clearer path to employment for the best of the best. We do this through "Easter eggs."

Easter eggs are hidden messages in your job ads. When an applicant spots them, you know you've got an invested, detail-oriented match. You can slip these in throughout an ad and then add a screening question or two into the process that tests the applicant. If they get it wrong, then the system can automatically decline them.

For example, we had a client who wrote in their job ad:

When we ask you how long we've been in business, we want you to put in 27, which is the wrong answer. Yes, we're making sure you're paying attention.

When an applicant applied, the ATS asked, "How long have we been in business?" Anybody who didn't put 27 or the actual answer was removed automatically.

Easter eggs test applicants. In the case of the question above it was testing candidates on whether or not they read the ad or researched the company. These don't have to be serious. You can have a lot of fun with your Easter eggs:

By the way, when we ask you to send us a link to the image, I want you to send us a link to your favorite Disney princess.

Then, when prompted later, the applicant can send the image.

There's only one real rule to Easter eggs: when you create them, make sure you are fair. The clues should be obvious enough that anyone paying attention can get them right. For the most part, we're using Easter eggs to help us eliminate the people who didn't take the time to read the ad. You don't want to make them so tricky you disqualify your best applicants—or so hard, those applicants lose patience and apply elsewhere.

And grade your Easter eggs based on the position you're hiring for. If you want to hire a midlevel manager, you can expect them to do more during the application process, including a detailed read of every line of your job ad. Whereas, if you're hiring for an entry-level position, don't make it so hard for them to get a job that they break down halfway through the process.

BUILDING A REPEATABLE PROCESS

When you're watching your favorite team play, there are always players on the sideline. They're on the bench waiting to be called into the game.

Whether you're watching football, baseball, basketball, soccer, or hockey, you've got those players on the sidelines, itching to get into the game.

Those players are there because teams need reserves. Imagine you're watching a game where a key player gets injured. If there is no replacement, the team suffers. In some sports, they may even have to play a man down. In those circumstances, everyone has to work harder, and it's far more difficult to win.

Well, the same thing happens in your business. Any time a great worker leaves for another opportunity—or any time you expand and need a great hire to fill a new position—you need someone who can come off that bench and fill in. If The Bench is empty, everyone works harder.

Most companies don't have a bench for people to sit on. There's no holding place to put applicants who are interested in working for you but who don't make the final cut for one particular position.

The question, then, is how you create a repeatable hiring process to fill those positions as soon as they're open.

Fortunately, your ATS can help here, too. All it takes is four steps:

1. Fill your bench by creating a *second* rejection step in your ATS hiring process. Instead of entirely dismissing those who fall short, you move them to The Bench, where you can call them up when needed.

2. Create a company culture newsletter that celebrates your company, team, and industry wins, and send it to everyone on your bench.

3. Keep them warmed up to work for you by introducing them to your team and your culture using email automation.

4. Keep the rookies on deck for those who are close to making the cut but might need more experience before joining your team.

The most important aspect of building a bench is to stay in communication. An email and/or text message list makes that easy. When a new position opens up, you can start your prospecting there first.

Filling Your Bench

To create your list, use your ATS the same way you might use a CRM. Today, most companies have email marketing lists with automated customer outreach to keep them interested in your company. An ATS can do the same for your recruiting bench.

Once you set this up, your ATS can automatically add applicants who receive a specific type of rejection to The Bench, so that all communication you need to share goes out to them.

Then, you just have to create that communication and let the system do the rest.

Create a Company Newsletter

As with the CRM customer lists, most companies also have a customer newsletter. We all know the value of sharing information about a company, its products, and its deals with customers. There's a reason this is such a popular form of marketing. It works.

And it works just as well with potential employees. An employee newsletter can answer all of the questions that job seekers have about your company. This is a great place to explain your Core to those who want to work for you. You can give The Bench company updates and share information about what it's like to work for you.

Suddenly, you have people who were already willing to apply now even more interested in getting a job with you. They know more about you now, and they're motivated to go that extra distance—finding those Easter eggs or getting those qualifications—if it means they can get that job on the next hiring go-round.

A newsletter is also an opportunity to share a "We're Hiring" message with your bench and employees. Letting your bench know that you want them to apply for a new opening is a great way to find people who may not be actively looking but are ready to make a change.

That's a lot of potential benefit—for what turns out to not be much work on your part. Putting together an employee newsletter does not have to be hard. Just brag about the things you're already doing. Bring your marketing team in to write a few short pieces that simply explain to your bench who you are.

You can use your newsletter to celebrate company milestones. If you have a company party, send out an email that says, "Wish you were here!" Include pictures of your team having a great time. If you're making a big impact in the community, get some photos, and have your marketing team write up a story about it in the newsletter.

We have one client right now where the owner sends a newsletter every week that includes anniversaries of employees, a section on all the people who got promoted, and a list of completed and upcoming projects. It gives everyone on The Bench a real sense of what they're missing out on—so they're primed to reapply when positions open up.

One client even targets their newsletter for a specific position. Because good foremen are so hard to find, they send newsletters to every person who has applied for that position in the past. They include information on what's going on for foremen at their company and the career path for anyone who gets hired.

You can also connect these stories back to your Core to show who you are and what you want to be known for.

These stories can help you attract the sort of perfect Core fit hires you're looking for. You want potential applicants to read and think:

"Hey, these guys are growing really fast." Creating vision alignment.

"Hey, this team is having a lot of fun." Showing values alignment.

"Hey, this company is really doing some cool things and making an impact." Demonstrating purpose alignment.

"...and I want to be a part of it."

Use your newsletter and your bench as a way to attract those people you want to attract. The messages you send to your company newsletter contacts should be informative and inspirational. Communicate with potential hires about all the amazing stuff you're doing. That way, they know just how great it would be to join the team.

To build a large bench, you have to move beyond the benchwarmers on your ATS list and reach out to "passive job seekers." According to the PricewaterhouseCoopers (PwC) Pulse survey, more than 50 percent of employees are looking to switch jobs at any time. According to Gallup's annual employee engagement survey, somewhere around 70 percent of employees are not engaged in their work. In other words, they'd like another job. However, many of these people will never visit a job board (only 3 to 5 percent ever do).

These individuals are perfect candidates for your bench. They're an ideal reader for your newsletter. All you have to do is reach out. You can do that by simply putting a pop-up on your careers page. That pop-up could say:

Hey, want to learn more about us? Don't see something that's a fit yet? Stay plugged in, and we'll share other job opportunities through our email newsletter.

With a bench stocked with former applicants and passive job seekers, you're now in a position to start hiring. Announce new positions (or just a general desire to hire new people) in the newsletter and wait for positive responses.

When you get an enthusiastic response from someone who loves what you're doing and really wants to work for you, respond immediately. Send that contact your list of open jobs. You can automate another email in a few days to find out if they're interested in talking about an open opportunity. And if you determine they fit your Core, get them in and figure out the best position for them.

Build Relationships with the Bench

An applicant newsletter is a powerful tool to keep your bench engaged for when you need to hire. But there's even more potential for your bench email list. This is your chance not just to advertise how great your company is but to build a relationship with the people on that list.

Every good coach knows that relationships are important not just to their starters but to the people on the bench. The benchwarmers must believe in the team, so they can jump into the game at the last moment and make an impact. The same is true for your bench.

People have so many things going on in their lives that it's easy to forget about you and disconnect from the interest they have in your company. To remind them and maintain that connection, you can automate an email campaign for everyone who joins The Bench.

You might have your marketing team write up ten short emails. It could look something like this:

1. Thank you for joining us

2. Check out our open jobs

3. Follow us on social media

4. Employee testimonial

5. Recruiting video

6. Our Core Story

7. Check out our Meet the Team page

8. Apply and share with a friend

9. Another employee testimonial

10. A message from the owner

Send these emails once a week.

We have one client with 150 employees who followed this process just as we describe it here. They drafted over a dozen emails and wrote a monthly newsletter that introduced their company to benchwarmers over a six-month period. Their systems delivered the materials automatically.

Within 18 months, they had over 3,000 people on The Bench from their ATS and another 2,000 people who signed up from their careers page.

For this massive bench, they spent $50 a month. And the next time they needed two dozen hires, they had more applicants than ever before—and the quality of those applicants had skyrocketed.

Keep Rookies on the Bench

People apply to jobs once they've been certified, finished school, or want to switch careers. But often, at that point, they don't have the required experience. They may have great potential, but they don't have the skills, training, and experience under their belts to perform at the same level as the rest of your team.

Most companies will take a certain number of these "rookies." They'll train them up and apprentice them until they reach that desired skill level—that's a farming approach to recruiting. But once the company is stocked with rookies, the rest of the top young talent is turned away—for obvious reasons. You can't have an entire team of rookies without enough mature, skilled veterans to train them up. The quality of your work would suffer.

Still, this leaves your company vulnerable. If you aren't grabbing every eager rookie out there, you will run into difficulties as your current team ages out and retires or moves elsewhere.

At that point, you'll regret letting those rookies get established somewhere else.

Your bench offers you an alternative. Instead of rejecting those rookies, you can put them on The Bench and send them your email campaigns over the next year or two. That way, when they have a bit more experience, they're primed to come back and join the team.

Let's say you connect with a young worker who recently graduated from an apprenticeship program. When they apply, they aren't right for a specific position with you. A year later, though, they've got more experience, and you've got an opening. If they've been receiving your emails, they're ready to reapply because they want to be part of your company.

You can do the same thing with people you have to let go. If you have to cut positions in a recession, you don't necessarily want to say goodbye to that talent forever. If you keep in contact, those people know when to reapply as new jobs become available—or when a position that's a better fit opens up.

At that moment, there's nothing better than getting someone who already knows your Core to make the team that much better.

THE EMPLOYEE REFERRAL PROGRAM

With all your new automated processes and hiring materials, you're now in a far better place to use one of the classic recruiting systems: the employee referral program. When an employee wants to refer your company to a friend, they now have a newsletter they can share or an email list they can sign their friend up for.

Providing these extra materials adds value to a valuable strategy—at least when done correctly. According to CareerBuilder, 82 percent of employers feel that employee referrals are higher-quality candidates that stay longer and are a better fit for the team.

The problem is generating more of those high-quality referrals. More hiring materials and automation help, but they aren't enough.

To begin with, we have to address motivations.

Ideally, it's best to motivate your team with something other than money. In the first place, money is often an ineffective motivator. According to Zippia, only 6 percent of employees refer for a cash reward. Additionally, if your only motivator is money, you're making that the primary incentive for your team. So, the next time someone offers *them* a dollar more per hour, forget about referrals, why would they stick around?

Even if they do, financial incentives for referrals can get pricey. Many companies that offer cash incentives find they have to give large sums—often several thousand dollars—to get referrals.

Now, this isn't always a bad deal for an employer. We worked with a company that calculated their advertising costs at $1,400 per new employee. Yet they were only offering $100 for a high-quality referral who lasted more than a month in their new position. The numbers didn't add up. If they were willing to drop $1,400 on job board ads, why not spend that money on their own people?

At the same time, remember that this is an employee *referral* program, not an employee *retention* program. Even if you've increased the amount significantly, don't hold the referral bonus back to make sure the employee works out. It's not the referrer's responsibility to ensure a new hire stays. If the person your employee referred gets the job and stays on for more than a week, your employee has done their job. You want to reward that behavior, not punish them for things beyond their control. Ultimately, if someone doesn't work out in the first ninety days, you need to look at your system to make sure it's eliminating people you should have never hired.

Regardless, whether you decide to give a big financial bonus or not, there are better ways to motivate your team to refer their friends. To find those improved incentives, you have to first understand the perspective of your employees.

What You're Really Asking Them to Do

Most people don't think switching jobs is fun. It takes effort to learn a new position, make new friends, and settle into a new culture. Why would your employees put their friends through this? Why ask them to leave a place they know to come to an unknown company where it could be worse? It's a gamble. And financial incentives make this a selfish impulse—asking a friend to take that gamble so they can make some money.

Your people don't want to risk a friendship or an awkward Thanksgiving with a family member—especially for some pocket change.

But what if you could motivate your team through more positive incentives, so that this didn't feel like a selfish act for a few bucks but a generous act that benefits everyone?

You can build an employee referral program that connects to your Core Values. Think about the behaviors you want your team to embrace and find incentives that speak to those values. For instance, a business that cares about family can offer more time with loved ones as an incentive.

We had a client years ago that had a lot of people doing shift work. Anybody who referred a friend got to pick their shifts for the next month—giving them more of that time with the people they cared about.

An incentive like this costs zero to the employer. And anyone who referred a friend could choose a three-day weekend or avoid working nights. They could go to their kid's recital or take that long weekend trip.

If your company is focused on long-term employment for your team and a strong future together, you can make the incentive an end-of-year bonus in that employee's retirement account. If you're all about fun, how about an extra week of vacation for a great referral or tickets to a great concert?

Not all of your employees will be motivated by what you offer, but if it's true to your Core, the right employees will be, and the wrong ones won't. And those right employees are more likely to refer more people who believe in the Core of your company. Suddenly, you'll have more right employees and fewer wrong ones.

TAKE ACTION

Automation makes your life easier, and there are three ways to do it:

1. Technology

2. Delegation

3. Build a Repeatable Process

If you want recruiting success you need an applicant tracking system. So, choose a platform that works for you and your team. Consider the journey you want to take your applicants on. Then build it.

Once your ATS is in place, get applicants to participate in the hiring process to make your life easier. Delegate the process to them by asking them questions that prequalify them to move forward. And keep in mind that one simple way to stand out is to communicate more frequently with potential job candidates.

Also, stay in communication with a company newsletter. Use email to build your bench with unsuccessful applicants and passive job seekers, who could eventually become great future workers.

When you're ready to move forward, automate with application screening questions. And use Easter eggs so you only let the serious applicants through.

Checklist

- [ ] Choose an ATS that your team will embrace and use. Make sure it includes the features you need to maximize its performance.

- [ ] Roll out your ATS by setting up automation and reporting so you know exactly how well it's working and the changes you need to make.

- [ ] Create a series of screening, or knockout, questions so your ATS can help you eliminate people who would waste your time. Add them to every open position and let the system help you make decisions on who to move forward with.

☐ Build your bench and develop email or text message campaigns to educate and engage those on it.

☐ Redesign your employee referral program so that the reward aligns with your company's Core.

5

INTERVIEW

I'd read countless business books; I knew I needed to get the "right people on the bus and in the right seats on the bus." I was also stuck...for years...unable to do this—year in, year out, getting by, but frustrated and stuck in the daily whirlwind.

Working with Ryan and the team at Core Matters helped us realize that we needed to adjust—OK, scrap and over-haul our entire hiring and onboarding process if we were to find and retain the right people. Ryan helped us real-ize that our Core Values weren't good enough either. Motivation, reliability, and cooperation were the bar and not aspirational. These values were going to get us B players, not A players. Once we understood what the "core" was and that it really, sincerely mattered more than we ever realized, we recognized that revamping our hiring process mandated creating a phase of the inter-view process that solely focused on determining if the job candidate was a culture fit for our team. By creating interview questions that weeded people out or moved them forward based on how well they fit and related to our Core Values, we found that we were finding people who craved to be part of our team. We found people who not only appreciated our Core Values, but who needed a company with our Core Values.

We now focus on finding people who believe in our work, our mission, our values, and who will get along with our existing A players. If they are a "culture fit," then we run them through another round of questions focused on determining whether or not they have the skills for the position. Guess what. For our entry-level positions, if they are a "core fit," we can teach them the skills from scratch. These adherents stick around, enjoy the work more, enjoy the office camaraderie more, and perform better for our clients.

—CHRIS SANFORD, owner of PuroClean Disaster Restoration Services, Providence, Rhode Island

Interviews hold a special place in the Core Fit Hiring System. What you learned in earlier chapters will help you attract better applicants who you'll be excited to interview. And in the chapters to come, you'll learn strategies to retain those better people on your team. Interviews are the pivotal point in the process.

Interviews are where you find out if you've got the right person or not. It's where you discover if you really have the A player who fits your Core you think you do.

Fortunately, there are strategies you can employ that get to the truth—strategies that will allow you to hire the best people every time.

TAKE YOUR TIME...BUT NOT TOO MUCH

Before we get to the truth, we have to talk about time.

Have you ever heard of speed dating? The idea is to sit down with someone for a few minutes and make the best impression you can. If it goes well, you agree to go on a real date later. But imagine if you used speed dating for marriage—fifteen minutes, and you decide if this person is *the one*. Then, it's off to the altar.

The idea is ludicrous, of course. You would never date someone for fifteen minutes and then propose. Such a decision is far too important to leave to a brief conversation. Yet, people interview for fifteen minutes all the time and then hire—even for some very key positions. How much can you learn about someone in that short time? How can you get to the truth with the clock ticking like that?

Under those constraints, no one should be surprised when a new employee doesn't work out after a few weeks.

Instead, you need a system that helps you take the right amount of time discovering who this person is without wasting any time or losing a great candidate. Remember, hiring is a lot like fishing. If you reel in a big catch too quickly, they will likely get away. If you leave them on the hook for hours, something else will gobble them up while you wait.

Your competitors are hungry to hire people too. If you're not paying attention to the people you already have in your pipeline, your competition will likely snatch them before you get around to them.

Fortunately, much of the work we've done already speeds up the process of getting those great applicants to you.

In this chapter, we'll cover each step of the Interview process, allowing you to integrate every component into your organization, hire the best candidates, build the most efficient use of your time, and put them on the course to stay for many years to come.

THE CORE FIT SCREEN

We call this process the Core Fit Screen. Much of what is ahead in each of the Core Fit Screen steps will seem strange compared to your current practices. Often, our clients are reluctant to fully integrate this system at first. They think it's too time consuming or their best candidates won't stick around through the process.

But the results don't lie. We've seen countless organizations transform by simply implementing this Interview process. One of the greatest examples was Matt. Before working with us, Matt put about thirty minutes into the entire process. It was fifteen minutes with him and fifteen minutes with one of his branch managers. Then, there was a decision.

He was hiring a ton of people, not because he was growing, but because he couldn't hold onto people.

He wasn't easy to win over to the Core Fit Screen process. He questioned us every step of the way. But now that he's implemented the system, he's hiring far fewer people—because each person he hires is a near perfect fit for his business.

That's what's possible with the right interview process.

Screening

As the name Core Fit Screen suggests, screening is a very important part of this process. The screening step includes everything we covered in the last chapter, as well as some nonautomated screening steps.

On a practical level, this step is about getting the must-have items on your list checked off before spending time with an applicant. But it's also about making a positive connection from the first contact and creating the opportunity for a relationship to grow from these brief encounters.

Before you schedule a full interview, you should have reviewed their application. The questionnaires or assessments should have been completed and reviewed. And all additional screening should be complete. That's what this step is all about. Screening is about getting first impressions out of the way. It's the "Do I see enough promise to invest in real quality time with you?" step of the process.

Think of this like the text chat you might have with someone before deciding to go on a first date. You'd rather review someone's profile and put a few minutes into a quick conversation to make sure you're a good match than jump immediately into an evening with someone you might not be compatible with.

This is the stage when you and the applicant work hardest to impress one another. It's important to remember that most people put more effort into the first impression than into any other meeting. Whether it's meeting a business partner, a date, or a new neighbor, first impressions matter.

You've already done a lot through automation to make the best impression. Now, it's time to see whether the impression the applicant is making lives up to reality.

And the best way to do that is by getting them on the phone. An extra phone call might strike you as a waste of time. After all, you're busy, so why spend an extra ten minutes chatting with people instead of bringing them in for interviews right away?

The answer is that this actually saves you time. So many people are going to apply for jobs at your company who don't meet your requirements. They're not a good culture fit, or they're not able to do the work. Or they have a schedule conflict. Or they're only applying until something else comes along. Or... you get the idea.

A simple phone call can tell you immediately if this person is a good match for your company, saving you hours of wasted time in interviews with people who shouldn't be there.

This cuts down the number of people you invest time in and gives you peace of mind knowing that you have the time to invest in them.

The point of the phone screen is to get that first sense of culture fit above all else. The rest of your screening process should have clarified if they have the skills and background for the job.

This step is meant to be quick. You don't need to grill the person, just spend ten minutes getting a sense of who they are.

During the call, ask them questions to learn about them and listen to what's not being said. Oftentimes, candidates will give you details about things that are important to them about their work or personal life. Explore these opportunities. Show genuine interest in them, and it will reward you later.

As you wrap up the call, schedule the next meeting immediately. Avoid an extra step of scheduling later. Book the next meeting while you have them on the phone.

There is another benefit to the screening call. It reduces applicants ghosting you later in the process. In a study conducted by

Indeed, 77 percent of job seekers say they've been ghosted by a prospective employer. Indeed also found that 76 percent of employers had experienced ghosting. Getting someone on the phone and committing to the interview can vastly reduce those numbers on both sides.

Show candidates that you're not like every other company. You reach out. You take an interest. This will get your applicants pumped for their interview. And you'll have a better sense of the person walking in the door. So that when the interview begins, you'll know exactly what you need to know about this person to see if they qualify for the position.

Culture Fit

As Chris at PuroClean discovered, your job is to make sure the candidate is the right fit for your team. They need the right mindset and they need the right skills to succeed in the job you're hiring them for. This is when the candidate is actually in the office for what you'd normally consider the "interview."

This is your moment to be selfish. As a business owner, it's your duty to find the people who best fit your company and do exactly what you need. Don't go into interviews looking to settle. Make the applicants qualify themselves.

If a candidate has culture alignment with your company, they will easily accept your vision. They're going to behave the way you want. And they're going to be excited to work for you every single day. They won't be looking for other opportunities because this is the job they've been looking for.

If the culture fit is right, you can check for position fit to make sure the individual will work well within that specific job you're hiring for.

When you put these pieces together—combined with the screening for skills and experience and your brief phone call with them—you have a clear picture of whether this individual truly qualifies for the work ahead.

In Chapter 1, we talked about the values at the Core of your company. Now is the time to put all that work to use to qualify candidates before making an offer.

Culture really can make all the difference for your team. We have a client that just hired an outside sales rep. They are a restoration company for water damage and mold.

The person they hired had no industry experience. But he really understood what their company was all about. There are training programs to bring someone like that up to speed with the work.

What you can't teach is culture. Someone either believes in it or they don't.

And you only want to hire those people who do believe in it.

We recognize that some positions require years of training and certification. However, when a candidate reaches out to you for an interview, you should already know if they have those basics. What makes the difference between the people who remain is largely cultural fit.

During this part of the interview, be sure to prepare questions that help you assess a candidate's alignment with your Core Values beforehand. You want to finish that interview able to answer these questions:

- Does this person buy into your vision?

- Are they aligned with your company's purpose?

- Are their values aligned with yours?

- Will this person fit in with the team?

Write down the questions and answers you'd like to see on a page. Then bring your script to the interview.

For instance, one of our clients has the Core Value "Fail Forward." Their question looked something like this:

Question to Ask the Interviewee

Tell me about a time you made a mistake that impacted your entire team. What happened, and how did you respond?

The response we're looking for:

We were working on a project, and I misunderstood the requirements. It wasn't until later in the day that I found out I had spent the last six hours doing it wrong. I went to my boss, admitted my mistake, and asked for support.

Here is what we're not looking for:

We were working on a project, and the team leader gave me the wrong instructions. Then later, he told me that I had been doing it wrong all along. I was upset, and the project ran late, but it was his fault for telling me the wrong thing.

You don't always have to be so direct with your questions. We have another client with a Core Value of "We Choose Growth." The company is obsessed with ensuring its team is always looking for new and better ways to work. As part of the Core Fit Screen, hiring managers ask candidates what books they're reading. They ask why they chose the book and what value it's brought to their lives. If someone doesn't read or share another way they're personally growing, they may not be the right person for them.

Culture fit isn't just about the present, though. You also need to know where this person is going and if they will grow with you.

During the interview, talk about both their personal and professional goals. This can be conversational and offers a great opportunity to understand their motives and goals.

If a candidate isn't a good culture fit, there's no reason to keep moving forward. Let them know the interview is over, thank them, and move on. If they do fit, then it's time to find out if they'll thrive in the position. You can roll right into the next step in the process or schedule it for another time. Either way, make the decision immediately and commit to it.

Position Fit

By now, Core Fit Screen should give you a pretty good idea whether the candidate is a cultural fit and has the potential to fit the position. After all, you've screened them for basic qualifications.

But now you have to find out if those qualifications truly speak to a position match. The aim is to place in front of them a few real-world scenarios common to that position and see if they have the skills and inclinations to handle them.

You'll want to prepare a few skill-related questions to make sure they know how to do the work. Can they demonstrate their knowledge and skill to function in the position?

You want to see those qualities you expect in your best people in those moments. Along with basic skills, you want to test for resourcefulness, permission to play values, and a willingness to ask for help.

There are a lot of questions you can ask to make them work through a situation they are going to be required to work in once they are employed.

One question we suggest for assessing position fit is, "What's the hardest part of doing this type of work?" If it's a job that requires physical labor and they complain about the toll it takes on their body, that may suggest they don't have what it takes to handle the job. Or, if their response isn't the hardest part, it may indicate that they don't have the experience they're selling you.

We've had some clients print out pictures and ask candidates to identify what is wrong in order to test how perceptive they are of errors related to their work. Others have tested candidates on how to perform a specific task or asked them to outline a simple process.

Another position fit test we recommend is to offer candidates partial instructions on a project and then leave for fifteen minutes.

There are usually one of two outcomes to this test. The candidate either sits there the entire time waiting for you to come back or they make an effort, ask for help, and do their best.

Knowing which type of person you're dealing with is very helpful when making that ultimate hiring decision.

Once a candidate proves they fit the company and the position, it's time to validate their answers by giving them a chance to prove they can really do the job.

If you're hiring technicians, it's time to bring them to your shop and see what they can do. Give them tasks that challenge them in different ways, such as having them diagnose a broken piece of equipment.

You can invite the candidate on a three-hour ride-along with one of the company's crews. The crew can be tasked with talking to the candidate and getting to know them so they can report on strengths and weaknesses, as well as how well the candidate fits in once they are outside the interview room.

This is the time to let those candidates call real customers and ask for payment or respond to emails from angry clients. They're no longer working in theory; you're testing if they can work in reality.

Too many companies have the same generic process for everybody. Don't give the same process to all your candidates. Tests should always align with the skills you need to identify.

We've seen companies hire skilled labor techs by giving candidates typing tests. But how often do labor techs need to type? And do you care if it's fast enough?

Each role in the company should have specific skill tests that match the requirements of that position.

If they will spend 99 percent of their time on the phone, test them on the phone. You will hear what the customer is going to hear. Role-play difficult customer situations to ensure that their likability isn't just based on in-person interaction.

Once you've validated a candidate can do the work, it's time to make a decision and hand them an offer.

Pullback Offer

When you follow the Core Fit Screen process, it's much easier to decide if you want to move forward with a candidate. But just before you commit, there's one more step. It's the Pullback Offer.

Back to our relationship analogy, the Pullback Offer is the moment before you propose. You've spent enough time together to know you want to be together, but this is still a big step—and it's easy for the little things to cause big problems down the line.

But before you slide the offer letter across the table, hold back a moment. If you've ever moved in with anybody, you know that there are often little things that irritate you about one another. These aren't deal-breakers, but it's better to come to an understanding beforehand so you don't get on each other's nerves.

If one of you wears shoes in the house and the other always takes them off in the entryway, that will create unnecessary conflict. What about which way the toilet paper goes? Or how you squeeze the toothpaste? These little things will add up, and they exist in the workplace too. So, wouldn't it be better to settle the matter before moving in?

We think so—hence the Pullback Offer. With the Pullback Offer, you make the candidate an offer, but before you move forward together, you have one last serious conversation.

Speak to the things that may be different from what they're used to. Think about the things that drive you crazy when you see people doing them.

Here are some basic things to get out of the way:

- How to approach deadlines. Are they strict or more of a recommendation?

- How to deliver work. Do we know when something is done, who defines done, and at what level of quality?

- How to communicate with each other. How do you communicate when things are going well? What about when they aren't?

- Discuss any red flags you saw during the interview (lack of eye contact, distractions, cell phone usage, etc.)

- Ask them for anything they have concerns about before moving forward.

Discuss your personality differences too. If you're not going to be their manager, include the manager in this conversation. Go over any assessments you've completed. Make sure to share your own results, too.

While those differences may be annoying at times, remember that differences aren't bad—they're just different. If you're outgoing and they're shy, it may cause problems later when they don't openly share. Address how those situations should be dealt with before they become an issue. You will avoid major conflicts later.

One of the best ways to approach the conversation is to fast-forward to the future.

Here's an example scenario for a "no micros" company during the Pullback Offer:

> **One of our Core Values is "no micromanagement." That means we don't hire micromanagers, and we don't hire people who want to be micromanaged.**

> **So pretend it's your seventh week with us, and you realize your boss is micromanaging you. You've finished onboarding, and you're still getting managed on every little thing.**

Ask the candidate: what do we do if that happens?

The obvious answer is to keep your head down and just keep the micromanager happy, but that's not what you want at your company. You want someone who's going to speak up. And the person you want to hire needs to know that's the expectation.

The aim here is to be straight with one another. If you invest six weeks of training and onboarding, it's better to have them come to you to clear the air if they start feeling this way. It's better than just quitting. If they know that up front, they just might come to you. You can dodge that bullet entirely.

In fact, you dodge bigger bullets still. A few years ago, an electrical contractor we worked with was hiring someone to be their office manager. He loved the top candidate. He thought she was amazing. She checked every single box.

He spent four hours over a couple of days digging into her skills, behaviors, and views. The whole time, he made it clear why the company did what it did and why he was so passionate about electrical work. He made it clear about the type of team he wanted to build, the type of customers they served, and why they served them the way they did.

Throughout the process, she always had the right answers and all the right skills. He was so confident, he almost felt he didn't need to do a Pullback Offer. But he followed the Core Fit Screen and did one anyway.

It was during this conversation that the candidate broke down. Through the tears, she admitted that she'd kept something back from him.

"I can't work the schedule you need me to work," she said.

The truth was she had a daughter and being able to pick her up from school was a priority. The job required staying in the office until after closing. The candidate was going to make excuses and keep working until she found a position that better fit her needs.

"I thought we were a match made in heaven," the company's owner said in shock.

"I'm sorry," she sobbed. "I can't do this to you. I get why you do what you do and why it's so important that you're there for your customers."

He was immensely disappointed, but in reality, he'd dodged a huge bullet.

That's the power of the Pullback Offer. It's a conversation that takes guts because we're not used to talking about these things. But if you're genuine and straightforward, you can weed out those final bad candidates and set those positive relationships with your new hires off to the best possible start.

LEAVING A GOOD IMPRESSION

The end of an interview is not only about wrapping up a conversation. Be intentional here too. There are two things you want to do for success later. First, you want to share, celebrate, and inform the candidate about the company.

Then, you want to set expectations for what will happen next. They should know what to expect and feel confident about joining your company.

During most of the Core Fit Screen, you're the buyer in the sales transaction. You get to be selfish and focus on what you need. As you end, it's time to switch again to being a seller. Use the last few minutes of the interview to tell people how great it is to work for the company. Leave a great impression. Do this whether you hire a person or not.

A good final impression goes a long way. Though that first impression is the most important, leaving things on a positive note confirms those positive opinions the candidate should already have. That motivates them for their first day and makes them eager to share their experience with others.

Whether they get a job or not, they might tell their friends who are your potential employees and customers.

If they aren't going to join the company, tell them why. If it makes sense, offer them options for staying in touch. Add them to your jobs newsletter. If they need training, tell them where to go. They could be a great future hire.

For those you do hire, there's further value here. Every great sales close ends with the next steps, and you want to have those in place, too. Set expectations. Prime your new hire for onboarding. It doesn't have to be more than saying, "We'll call you within forty-eight hours." Then, follow through on your promise to call them. Don't leave them wondering what the next steps will be.

TACTICS FOR INTERVIEW SUCCESS

The Core Fit Screen above details how to find the best hires and bring them into the team with the least amount of time and effort on your part. It's designed to bring the best applicants forward and leave everyone with a positive impression of the experience.

But that doesn't mean that the process takes care of everything itself. There are some further tactics you can employ to give yourself the right information and to ensure you're making the best decision.

Preparing Interview Questions

When interviewing, do not focus on past performance. It's not a good indicator of future success. You read that correctly. We don't believe past performance is a good way to determine if they will perform for you. You have no idea how toxic their last employer was or how laid back their last manager was in managing performance. There are simply too many variables that you don't know. So it's best to see how someone performs now and in your office.

Developing a set of interview questions can be a surprisingly complex process—far too much so for the scope of this book. Suffice to say here, there are five types of interview questions we encourage everyone to use, beyond the basic questions that everyone asks.

- Role Playing

- Scenario

- "Tell Me about a Time..."

- Process Focused

- Give the Answer First

In role-playing questions, you create hypothetical scenarios to measure a candidate's potential future behavior. You might, for instance, play the role of a customer with the candidate acting in their future position. As the customer, you could sound frantic or offer limited information. How does the candidate respond to this?

Similar role-plays can involve you taking on various positions—a manager or a colleague—under various difficult circumstances.

With scenarios, you're still dealing with hypotheticals, but you're asking the candidate to give their honest opinion about very difficult situations with no clear right answers. You might ask how they'd respond if a coworker arrived thirty minutes late and left thirty minutes early one day. Would they mind their own business, confront the employee, or talk to a manager? What about if an employee took credit for the work they'd done or if they disagree with how their boss is handling a particular situation? There are plenty of reasonable answers to these questions, but you want to know how this particular candidate would respond (and whether that matches the values of your company).

"Tell me about a time..." questions move into reality and ask how the candidate has behaved in the past. Instead of asking, "How would you...," you say "Tell me about a time...

- ...You had to deliver bad news to your boss."

- ...You made a mistake that affected the whole team."

- ...You realized you were unqualified for a task."

These are meant to be uncomfortable and to put the candidate on the spot while you grade how they dealt with difficulties in the past. Make sure that once they've answered you that you're able to bring that response to the realities of joining your team.

If they didn't share something that would work well in your company, address it now because that's a red flag.

Process-focused questions are not really questions so much as experiences you put the candidate through to see how they react in real time. You might play a card game and change the rules two minutes in to see what they do about it. Do they remain silent? Do they call you out? These questions can also be planted when you're validating them on the job. Simply add a few challenges to their work to see how they respond as they crop up.

Finally, with give-the-answer-first questions, you check the candidate's preparation and attention. You might tell them what you want to hear at the end of the interview in the job ad or an early automated email. You could ask them to watch a three-minute video before the interview and then ask them a couple of questions from that video. This way, you know if they really prepare and take in the information you share with them.

A good interview has a mix of all these types. Together, they allow you to develop a clear portrait of how the candidate will respond to the job.

Getting Honest Answers

The key to any good interview is getting honest answers to your questions.

Unfortunately, that's often the hardest part of the job. Anyone walking into an interview is incentivized to distort the truth for their benefit. Applicants naturally want to make themselves look good so they can get the job.

For that reason, almost everyone has a script in their head that they've practiced over and over again. They've anticipated your questions, and they've crafted their answers to make them appear as positive as possible. The last thing they want to tell you is the complete, transparent truth.

Luckily, there are strategies you can use to get to that truth, whether the candidates you're interviewing intend to share it or not. We learned these strategies from Chris Voss's book *Never Split the Difference*, where he talks about negotiating and how to get everyone on the same page.

Start with encouragers. Encouragers include a lot of verbal and nonverbal communication that "encourages" the person you're interviewing to open up and reveal more. This can be as simple as raising an eyebrow at the right moment, smiling and nodding along to a story, or adding an enthusiastic "right" or "oh yeah?" from time to time.

Nearly as subtle as encouragers is mirroring. This involves repeating a keyword the person you're interviewing says.

If you want to hear more about a disagreement an applicant mentions they had with a former boss, drawing out a whole new question can put the applicant on guard and leave them running for their script. Repeating what they say with a quick "disagreement?" lulls them into elaborating and revealing the truth.

Then there are mislabels. People can't help but correct you. It's in their nature. If you say something that's wrong, people want to jump in and state the truth—even when it isn't in their interests.

You might mislabel something about an applicant's résumé, pushing them to correct you—and reveal the truth behind a situation. For example, if they claim to have two years of experience in a role, see how they react when you suggest they're new to this work.

They'll either prove they know their stuff, or they'll reveal they've exaggerated. Either way, you end up with the truth.

These strategies may sound too simple to work, but that's exactly why they do.

Objectivity over Relatability

Have you ever met an applicant, and you clicked in the first couple of minutes? You share a common experience, and once identified, it is like you've known each other for years. In such moments, your impulse is clear: this is the one. The interview can be over before it even really started.

Sometimes this impulse is correct—but not always. People tend to hire people like them. It's human nature. The problem is that, generally, you don't need another you on the team. You need someone who complements you.

Strong, cohesive teams require balance, and balance is only possible when you have different personality types on the team. In other words, sometimes the best hire is someone you don't click with immediately.

The best way to be objective and make the best hiring decisions is to decide up front what answers are ideal for the questions you're asking. How you interpret questions will always involve an aspect of personal bias and subjectivity, but you can be more objective with a rating system.

Let's say you ask a candidate about one personal goal they'd like to accomplish in three years. There really is no right answer. Answers can range from having no goals on the low end of the continuum to an ideal goal of wanting to move into management at your company. In between, you have a whole spectrum of answers that may start at the low end of just having a goal. The middle point might be a goal that is outside work but aligns nicely with their advancement. And higher end goals might be more work focused—perhaps qualifying for an important certification or taking business classes. Rate each answer on a scale of 1 to 3, indicating where their answer falls on the spectrum.

**Consider how you want them to answer,
not what you want them to answer.**

After a series of interviews for a position, add the scores and hire the person or people with the best score. That doesn't mean that complementary personalities count for nothing. You can give a score for that, too, but it should only be one part of the equation. If the scores elsewhere don't add up, they aren't right for the job.

Rock Star or Superstar?

Before you set out to implement the Core Fit Screen for a specific position, you must get clear on what kind of person you want to hire. In particular, you need to know if you're looking for a Rock Star or a Superstar.

This concept comes from the book *Radical Candor* developed by Kim Scott. According to Scott, both roles are assets to a team. Neither is better or worse. They're just different.

Rock Stars are the rocks of your team. They're the foundation. They're people you can rely on when times get tough. They're reliable because they want to be excellent at their current job. They're the ones you tap on the shoulder when you need someone to train the new employee. They typically don't want to move up or take on more responsibility. That means they're not the type you're going to promote. They're best staying in that role long-term.

Many employers love these people so much that they want them to be managers. But once promoted, they aren't as effective as they were in their previous position. This dilemma touches on the Peter Principle—the idea that people within an organization are promoted until they reach a level at which they are incompetent.

No matter how talented someone is in a position, that doesn't make them a talented manager—nor does it make management appealing to them. A Rock Star's dream is to work at their current job. They want to excel and keep getting better at their current role. They love the idea of knowing that they do it better than anyone else. They're not interested in new roles or responsibilities.

Superstars are the opposite of Rock Stars. They want a growth trajectory. They are looking to grow in new projects, areas, and skills. They want to keep up with the times, so they're always relevant. Superstars want to learn and grow in new ways. If they don't move up, they move on.

Superstars are the people who come to you asking for a raise, more responsibility, or to take the lead on the next project. If you enable their growth, they might positively change everything, including your processes, systems, and team, because they always look for a better way to do things.

Superstars are the future leaders of your company. You need them, but you don't need as many of them as your Rock Stars.

Keep all this in mind in your interviews. We've found that Superstars interview incredibly well. They know what you want to hear. They will tell you all the right things. They're used to switching jobs, so they have a lot of practice in interviews. Rock Stars, on the other hand, may not interview as well. They can be nervous or even give incomplete answers. They don't want change, so they don't interview as often. They rarely look for jobs unless the right opportunity comes along or they're forced to.

It's easy to be wooed by Superstars. Employers meet them and get excited. But if you hire every Superstar you interview, very soon you'll experience retention issues. Either those Superstars won't prove adept at the job they have now or they'll move on to the next big thing before you have a chance to promote them. Recognizing Superstars and Rock Stars is extremely valuable in the interview. You'll be able to create the right balance between those born for a particular role and those you want to cultivate as leaders.

The Wait

Imagine you've just become engaged. You planned the whole evening—the dinner, the candles, the walk on the beach—and you went down on one knee and proposed.

And then, after your future spouse said yes, you just... disappeared.

After that dramatic moment, you tell your fiancée that you'll see them at the wedding, and then you just don't communicate.

Sounds like a terrible idea. Yet, it's the policy that most companies follow with their new hires.

With the interview well organized, the right questions asked, and the best decision made, there's just one thing left to do: wait. Rarely, if ever, does someone start a new job immediately. They must go home, tell their partner, turn in their notice, and see their old job through for a week or two.

Almost every company does nothing but wait during this period. But this is truly a crucial period. During this time, anything can happen—including losing your new hire entirely. They might take your offer letter back to their current boss and use it for leverage. They could get home and tell their spouse, who disagrees with this decision. They could have cold feet and change their mind.

This risk is exacerbated by the actions of the employer—or rather, the lack of action. What tends to happen after an offer on the employer's end is silence. The employer hires the candidate and thinks they are coming back in a few weeks. Until then, they forget about their new employee.

But this period can be a tense one for your new hires. There can be doubt, uncertainty, and hesitation. Each day, as they say goodbye to coworkers and prepare for a major shift, they wonder whether they made the right choice.

Employers ignore this difficult period at their own peril.

Recently, Ryan went to lunch with one of his clients. They're long-term skeptics of doing anything during The Wait. "What's the point?" they've argued.

They just found out the hard way. At lunch, they told Ryan they'd hired three all-star technicians. They were all meant to start this past Monday.

When that Monday rolled around, the company got one call. One of their technicians was sick and wouldn't be in for a week. The other two simply never called or showed up at all.

Don't let this happen to you anymore. Take advantage of this time and start onboarding them while everyone is waiting.

To ease the mind of your new hires and keep their motivation high, you can build a process to communicate with them. Here's an example.

- Before they leave the interview, ask them if they need to give notice to their current employer. Guide them through this new stage in their life. If they're nervous, give them the confidence to have the conversation by role-playing it with them.

- Find out their plans and support them through the process. Changing work is a stressful time. Make it easy for them.

- Think about the emotions you want them to feel

during this time: happy, excited, relieved, etc. Build your process around that.

- They're going to talk to others about your hiring process. What do you want them to say? Create an experience for them that supports this.

Ultimately, you want new employees to know their new boss cares and is there for them.

Imagine how they'll feel when fifteen minutes before they turn in their notice, they get a text from you like this:

Hey, good luck with the conversation this morning. I'm rooting for you. I'm excited to have you join the team!

Then, a couple of hours later you send them this:

How did the conversation go?

It makes accepting a dollar an hour more from their current employer when their employer begs them to stay less appealing when they're reminded of the great opportunity ahead of them. And it takes little effort to do this and solidify a new relationship.

Once they've put in notice, you can maintain this connection as you start onboarding. When you're processing their new-hire paperwork, setting up their accounts, or even ordering their equipment, keep them in the loop.

Hey, just wanted to let you know we have your new email set up, and the team is getting your new work computer ready to go. I'm excited to have you join the team!

There's plenty of room here to express how much you care about the people in your company. You can send a handwritten note, a gift box, some company swag, or a couple of movie tickets. Most of these gifts can be automated to be sent out during The Wait, but they mean a lot to the people receiving them.

Small gestures let new employees know you're excited to have them. This keeps them from disappearing after they've accepted, and it doesn't take much, just a bit of intentionality.

You can also add new hires to internal email lists. Then once they check their email, they're already in the loop about what's happening.

Being intentional during The Wait will separate you from the rest of the companies your new hires have worked for. These actions cement the value you place on your relationship with your team and how interactions will go moving forward. You want to instill total confidence in them and show them you want them there.

When you invest these twenty extra minutes in solidifying a relationship up front, you will have an easier time onboarding and retaining later.

TAKE ACTION

Standardize the Core Fit Screen for all new hires. Before you interview, prepare interview scripts. Consider what questions and answers you'd like to see at each step of the interview—Screening, Culture Fit, Position Fit, and Pullback Offer. It will help you and your team remain objective.

Be clear on whether you need to hire a Rock Star or a Superstar *before* starting the interview. And watch out for flags that you're interviewing the wrong type of person.

Consider how you'd like to communicate with new hires during The Wait and how you could automate or delegate this process. Implement structures to make sure tasks get handled for each new employee before day one.

Refer to the following checklist to maximize your interview experience and results.

Checklist

- ☐ What roles are you currently hiring for? Consider the questions you'll ask and the answers you want to hear from candidates. Create scripts for your interviews. Follow the same process regardless of the role.

- ☐ Set up a phone screening process that is incredibly responsive. Call an applicant within one hour of receiving their application if you want the best chance to interview them.

☐ Identify how you will assess someone for a position fit. Build out scenarios before the interview.

☐ Build out your communication templates and campaigns for The Wait before you have someone enter it. Keep them engaged during this time.

☐ Train and involve everyone in your company who conducts interviews to develop and use these new processes.

6

ONBOARD

A janitorial company came to me because they were experiencing low engagement, high turnover, and zero growth. Their solution was extremely ambitious: an intensive apprenticeship program.

It was a great idea, but it was impractical. Their team was struggling now. They didn't have time to build that program. What they needed was to make sure they hired the right people and those people stuck around.

I reviewed their hiring process, and everything seemed to be in order. They were very thorough. Then I looked at their onboarding. It turned out that once someone was hired, they were just thrown into the deep end. The only onboarding offered was a forty-five-minute orientation, and sometimes, even that was skipped.

It was a jarring experience for the new hires who came in expecting a really hands-on approach based on their interviews.

Simply upgrading the onboarding system to provide that missing support changed everything. Suddenly, those great hires started sticking around—and the company started growing again.

—JEREMY

Hiring great people doesn't amount to much if they leave in six months. To avoid massive churn on top talent, you must get your onboarding right. According to a study by Gallup, a good onboarding process improves new employee retention by 82 percent and productivity by over 70 percent. The same study reveals that employees with good onboarding experiences are eighteen times more committed to their employer.

The aim of onboarding is deceivingly simple:

Pass ownership of the role from you to your employee.

While new employees may know how to do their job, they don't know how to do it *your* way. Those early weeks of employment are about teaching new employees how communication, processes, and team dynamics work at your company.

This is true of every onboarding program. The aim is always to teach the employee the ins and outs of their role, so you don't have to do the work for them.

But onboarding can be more than that. Along with passing ownership of the role along, you can get your new employees to *lead* the onboarding themselves—requesting what they need so they can deliver for you at the highest level and with the least oversight.

To do this, you need an employee-led onboarding system. And when you install the right system, you save time, provide better training, allow employees to truly own their role, and create a team of loyal, independent workers.

It's a win for everyone—but only if you do it right.

OTR^2: THE PURPOSE OF EMPLOYEE-LED ONBOARDING

We want each and every employee to do two things, own the role and own the results, or as we call it, OTR^2. Imagine having a whole team of independent workers who are crystal clear on how performance is measured, take responsibility for their tasks, show initiative when they have questions, and always hold themselves accountable. Such a team would know what it takes for them to win and would put themselves in charge of their performance.

For overworked entrepreneurs, a team of these employees feels like a pipe dream. So much of your time is spent putting out other people's fires. A world in which every member of the team reaches for the fire extinguisher first—it's almost too much to hope for.

But an employee-led onboarding system can absolutely make this a reality.

If you're doing what you need to be doing to get an employee to OTR[2] in the first ninety days of their career with your company, you create the ideal circumstances for them to live and breathe that responsibility the entire time they work for you.

And if you follow the advice in this chapter, by twelve weeks, your new hire is demonstrating ownership of both of these factors. When they do, their results will be exponentially greater—and they will require far less attention from you.

Own the Role

When someone owns their role, two things happen.

First, they stop needing support from the rest of the team. They can figure out challenges on their own. They know who to go to when they have questions, but they don't need much help to do their job. Second, when a problem does occur, they don't need their boss to fix it. Once an employee does these two things, they can really step into their role.

To do that, they have to inject their own personal touch into the position. Owning the role means they've made it their own. Everybody's got a slightly different work style. You can have an extrovert and an introvert in the same role, and they'll own it in their unique way.

That doesn't mean everyone is suited for a particular job or that a new hire doesn't have to follow your processes. It simply means that once you have the right person in the role, they can follow your system with their unique skills and personality. An effective employee-led onboarding process focuses on empowering them to seize ownership of the position you know they can fill (while also providing you the opportunity to reevaluate if they truly fit or not).

Own the Results

Owning the process is a start to preparing a new employee for success, but it's only half the equation. They have to own accountability for the results too.

In many companies, employees have no idea what impact their work has on the business. The onboarding process helps them understand what acceptable results are, how their role impacts the company, and what they can do to affect it. When they know how crucial their work is, they can take responsibility for the outcomes of it.

An employee who owns their results stands behind them—good or bad. They take pride in their successes. They admit their failures when something goes wrong. They ask for help. And, if they don't hit their numbers, they accept it without blame. An employee who owns their results adheres to the metrics you set for them. If they hit five and the rest of the team hit seven, they work to improve and catch up. They understand where they're at and the impact it has on everyone.

Employees can't do this without knowing exactly what is expected of them and why. If you don't provide them with the information they need to measure their performance, they'll be shooting in the dark. They'll have no idea what it takes to win because they won't understand how you're keeping score.

Imagine you've got a new employee whose job is to bowl. They're required to roll the ball down the lane and get as many strikes as they can. But when they step up to the lane, they find out there's a giant curtain obscuring their view of the pins.

They don't know what they're aiming at, and they don't know how many pins they hit every time they roll the ball.

This may sound ridiculous, but this is exactly how most employees feel when they don't know what you expect.

But what if you just remove the curtain? What if your employees could see the pins and aim for them? What if they knew when they were bowling strikes and when they were throwing gutter balls? And what if a little coaching is all they needed to start hitting more pins?

Owning their results isn't something they do on their own. They need your support and guidance. Once they can clearly see how you're keeping score, it's much easier for them to aim and win.

AVOID THE TRAINING TRAP

To build a team that can OTR^2, you'll need an onboarding process that prioritizes independent development and communication. It's likely that onboarding will also include training for certain components of the job, but beware, focusing on training above all else can be a trap.

Training can be an excuse for poor leadership or poor employee performance. Less discerning leaders think if they train a person, that person will magically do what is needed.

But that's not what training is for. Training won't fix character issues or a culture mismatch. You can't train away someone's negative mindset. In the bowling story above, if we sent the disenchanted new employee to training, it wouldn't have changed their engagement or ability to perform.

We've worked with companies that hire inside sales reps to pick up the phone and call leads or past customers. No amount of training will fix the person who walks in and looks at the phone like it's a fifty-pound dumbbell. That is the wrong person in the wrong seat. Employers think they can give new hires a bit of basic sales training and a new CRM or headset. And then...problem solved! Except it doesn't work that way—not if you're looking for growth and less oversight on your part.

Ryan has experienced this phenomenon himself. Back in his corporate days, he had an outbound sales rep named Steve.

Steve came in full of excitement to be working in sales. Yet his numbers never quite matched that enthusiasm. Every time Ryan asked what was wrong, there was always an excuse. At first it was the notepad or a lack of training in one skill or another. Then it was the headset, the leads list, or even the desk.

Eventually, Ryan realized that it had nothing to do with tools or training. It was the mindset Steve brought to sales. He just wasn't a good fit for the position, and there was nothing Ryan could do about that.

Training is valuable in two main scenarios: teaching the key components of a task or role and helping someone learn a new skill. For everything else, training is a Band-Aid at best.

So, while training is certain to be a part of your onboarding, you shouldn't build your program around it. Instead, you need an onboarding program that allows new employees to get the training they need to solve their own problems, while equipping them to OTR^2.

STARTING OFF ON THE RIGHT FOOT

Before you set up an employee-led onboarding system, make sure you start your onboarding right. It's worth pointing out that onboarding began when your new hire was applying for the job. From that moment on, you've been establishing the type of relationship you want with this person—the type of boss you are and the type of culture your company has. Every detail—from how fast you responded the moment they applied to your focus and preparedness in the interview, and how you communicated through the crucial wait period—has been important.

You want to continue creating a positive experience for your new people when they arrive to start their job.

There are two key components to a great first impression:

1. Setting expectations, accountability, and measures of success

2. Celebrating new team members

If you get both right, you will have a committed new employee ready to embrace onboarding.

Setting Expectations for Success

Employers often start new employees with little information about the job they just started. They don't know what they're responsible for, what the expectations are, how they'll be held accountable, or how they'll know they've succeeded. In other words, they don't know the rules of the game your team is already playing.

So, the first thing you have to do is to explain the rules to your new hire. Of course you'll check in with them, but you also must respect their intelligence and their ability to succeed. Let them know they can lead the relationship and ask for training and support on their terms.

As part of setting the rules, always share what you expect. These expectations should be reasonable. Never expect massive results in the first ninety days. Onboarding is a time for everyone to learn.

These expectations can begin with your Core Fit Profile. Share that document with them and explain why it's so important. By bringing the Core Fit Profile to the forefront of onboarding you show them what really matters to your organization.

At the same time, make clear that you don't expect them to be incredibly productive in the first two weeks, but you still expect them to work. In fact, they will learn more by working. Onboarding gives them space to acclimate and learn your way of doing things *while* they ramp up and start producing.

Before you send them off, lay out the metrics you'll use to monitor their progress. Some companies call them KPIs, scorecards, metrics, or targets. Call them whatever works for you. These are the targets that you want a new hire to hit by the end of their first ninety days.

Your metrics will depend on the industry and position. Metrics for entry-level, general labor positions may include attendance and customer satisfaction numbers. For sales, it might be the number of dials per day and speed to answer calls. For field technicians, you may track the amount of work performed or number of customer callbacks.

Whatever your metrics, your new hires need to be very clear on what targets you expect them to hit and by what specific dates. There needs to be buy-in and acceptance. If you tell someone to do something and they don't understand why it should be done, odds are it won't get done—or it will get done poorly.

Make sure metrics are for a small number of tasks. Even for a leader, two to three tasks are enough to start. If new hires are made accountable for more than a few metrics at a time, they will not remember them. And if they miss one, they'll likely miss them all.

When you introduce new employees to the metrics they'll be measured by, let them know that their onboarding is a collaborative effort. If they need anything, they can always speak up. Reassure them that if they're feeling lost or confused, they can discuss it with you, and you'll work on it together. The aim is always to make this feel like a partnership. You are in this together—you want them to succeed as much as they want to.

This is also a moment to express the independence you want them to feel in the role. You want them to know they can take risks. Reasonable risk-taking is a quality you want to encourage because when people take risks, they challenge assumptions and make the business run better.

In the onboarding ahead, you'll have plenty of opportunities to break down mistakes and figure out together if they were on the employee side or a process that needs improvement. The key is you'll review and solve it together.

This offer of flexibility must come from a genuine place. If your new team member reaches out for help, only to hear that no one is available, they'll be more frustrated than they would have been in the first place. It's always better to slow down onboarding and set your future employees up for long-term success.

Let's say you hire someone with experience. An effective onboarding task in their first twelve weeks might be having them assist a mentor while they learn about the inner workings of your company, such as operating procedures and the culture.

This was precisely what one of our clients did. They run an electrical contracting company. For the first four weeks after they hired a new electrician, they would have their new hire ride along with a master electrician.

Over the course of that time, the master electrician would onboard their new colleague and teach them every aspect of the job. That included basics like how to submit payroll and who to go to for supplies, but it also went into some of the intangibles. The master electrician would show how they did work at that company and how to interact with customers.

This was a customer-facing job, and the owner had found in the past that many new hires came in with bad habits. Simply working alongside an established member of the team for a few weeks introduced all the right habits—so that when their new team member finally got their own truck, they truly understood what it meant to work for that company.

Meeting Your Own Expectations

Imagine Jimmy, the newest accountant at World's Best Services, Inc., comes into his first day of work at the office. His supervisor greets him beside a desk that is buried under a pile of unsorted documents.

"Hi, boss," Jimmy says, eyeing the tower of boxes threatening to topple over his new workspace.

The supervisor smiles enthusiastically. "Sorry about the mess. We've known for the past couple of weeks that you were joining us, and we figured you could handle all of this once you came. Hit the ground running, you know?"

Jimmy nods slowly. "I could start by logging into my computer—"

"Well, no. IT is a little behind, so your login isn't active yet."

"Right..." Jimmy sets his bag down. "I guess I'll start with these papers then."

The supervisor pats him on the shoulder. "That's the spirit! We're so glad to have you on the team." He walks back to his office, leaving Jimmy alone with the backlog of work that needs to be done. "Oh, and one more thing!" He sticks his head out of his office. "Careful about those boxes. Your insurance doesn't kick in for another ninety days, so it will be a problem if you get hurt."

Jimmy is left standing there and thinking, *They knew I was coming and didn't bother setting anything up. My desk is a mess. I might die under those boxes. Nobody actually cares that I'm here. And I don't even know how they want me to do it.*

What does Jimmy do? He sits down at his desk, pushes the papers to one side, and starts scrolling through his phone for new job listings.

This is the reality for so many employees. Many employees show up on the first day, and their boss isn't prepared. The message that sends—right on day one—is that this job just isn't that important. And the person working that job isn't important either.

If you're going to hold your new hires accountable and set expectations, you have to do the same on your end.

Ensure processes are in place ahead of time to handle all the tasks for setting up their first day. Create a checklist of what you need to do *before* someone's onboarding and start working on it as soon as they accept the offer.

Celebrate New Team Members

Often new hires are told they are appreciated and a celebrated member of the team, but the actions of business owners suggest the opposite is true. The onboarding process reveals that the company is either disinterested or disorganized. One thing is for certain: they are not set up for employee success.

If you want your new employees to succeed, you must take your time and celebrate them—and then you have to prove you mean it.

If a new employee doesn't feel like they're winning, they won't want to keep playing. You want them to feel welcome. You want them to understand that they're important.

No matter their role, you want new hires to be excited to be there, and you want them to know that you're excited they are there. You hired them, and they are an amazing addition to the team. They are coming to work for you. That's worth celebrating!

Think of what it feels like for most employees when they show up on the first day. Even if things are better organized than they were for Jimmy, they walk in and it seems like no one cares. Most people don't notice them; it's just another day for the team already in place.

But for that new hire, this is a big day. It could be the start of the best job of their life. They're only going to feel that way, though, if you draw attention to that fact.

Stop throwing parties only when people retire or leave. Throw them when new people show up. It's amazing what this small gesture will do for everyone. This isn't just valuable for the new employee. If you tell the team you hired another Rock Star, it boosts morale across the company. Suddenly, the team is excited to meet the person who will push this company to the next level. And when the new person sees that reaction, they'll know they made the right choice.

Celebration cuts through the fearful side of taking a new job. When employers say, "Here's the keys, good luck!," it throws people into survival mode. That's not a pleasant experience, to put it mildly. And it isn't a productive one either.

That doesn't mean you should throw a party every few weeks when a new member joins the team. That wouldn't be a good use of time or resources, and it also wouldn't motivate every new employee.

When it comes to celebrating a new hire, take into account how that person is motivated. Not all people want to be celebrated with a big party. Curate a lineup of options that you can choose from.

If you used the prehire personality assessments discussed in Chapter 3, the report you get will tell you how to celebrate your new employee in a way that energizes them.

Generally, you'll always hire one of four styles of people, each with their preference for how they'd like to be acknowledged and celebrated:

1. Always in Charge

2. Life of the Party

3. Super Patient

4. Rule Follower

Always in Charge is someone who dominates the conversation. They want everyone to know that they are there. Being a dominant type, they will likely tell you what they want. They will want to be the center of attention and meet everyone in one giant swoop. High dominants will want the party, so they can immediately show they're ready to take the lead.

The Life of the Party also likes a big party. As the name suggests, they are your extreme extroverts. They love people and are able to keep the conversation, and the party, going. Still, a high extrovert likes attention and has no problem being seen, so make them feel special by making an obvious fanfare that they have arrived.

That big celebration isn't such a great idea for the Super Patient types, though. These people are a bit more methodical. They want a systematic way of getting to know everyone. So, take your Super Patient new employees out to lunch each day of their first week with a different team member, so they can get to know them at a slower, quieter pace.

Last but not least, you've got your Rule Follower. Unsurprisingly, they want to follow the rules. But they also like to set them. Give them a list of what celebrations are available at your company and let them choose. These types tend to like a quieter acknowledgment but leave it up to them.

If you aren't sure where a new employee fits—especially if you haven't run a personality assessment—just ask. Establish a menu of celebration options that are easy to do and budget friendly. Then, let each person choose the celebration that will make them feel truly welcomed.

Setting expectations and celebrating is very important throughout the onboarding process. During the first two weeks, you'll do more in these areas. Then, as your new employee gets the hang of things, it's time for the rest of your 2:4:12 Launch.

THE 2:4:12 LAUNCH

With first impressions covered, and your new hire ready to tear into their new position, it's time to use that employee-led onboarding system. We call the first ninety days the **2:4:12 Launch**.

Each key point in the onboarding should correlate to a particular question:

- **Two Weeks**: Can they fit our culture?

- **Four Weeks**: Can they do the job?

- **Twelve Weeks**: Can they win in this role?

Hit those targets, and by the end of week twelve, you've got someone ready to own their role and their results for years to come.

The First Two Weeks

When a new hire joins your team, the first two weeks is the "get to know each other" phase. As we've already discussed, you're setting expectations and celebrating their addition to the team.

During the first two weeks, as the employer, keep your own expectations around performance low. They're drinking from a fire hose right now. They're learning your way of working. They're figuring out processes and communication styles. They're absorbing the org chart, the hierarchy, and the company politics. Your expectations should focus on the basics. Are they showing up on time? Are they engaging with fellow team members?

During this time, you also want to review prehire assessments with the new employee if you've used them to help them quickly understand and navigate different behaviors, personalities, and communication styles.

It's a lot—and placing expectations for major output on top of everything else can feel very overwhelming.

Understandably, this can be a bit frustrating on your side. After all, you hired someone to fill a need. You've gone through a long process to find the right person. You want them productive as soon as possible.

But you can't expect a brand-new employee to work at or come close to the same level as a seasoned member of your team. It's unrealistic, and it puts too much pressure on your new hire. Under those circumstances, you can burn them out before they even settle in.

According to an article published by HumanPanel, people need five to eight months before they can produce as much as a seasoned team member. So if they produce at 25 percent of your target in the first thirty days, they are doing well.

They'll fill the rest of their time working with mentors and fellow team members to learn the job. You can set scavenger hunt tasks around the shop to help them settle. You might ask them to introduce themselves to the person at the front desk and ask a couple of questions or to sit in on a meeting outside their own team. They can fetch supplies for the crews to get to know more people. You can send them out to lunch with suppliers or spend half a day with dispatch. Or simply have them work closely with a mentor.

Importantly, you should leave these tasks up to the new hire. They'll decide when they're ready to take those activities on. Some may go through the list of requirements in a couple of days. Others may take the entire two weeks. It's their responsibility to get through it all.

Questions to Ask at Two Weeks

At the end of the first two weeks, your new team member will have hit the first of their milestones. Now it's time to sit down with them and have a short conversation.

The conversation at two weeks is meant to assess how well they fit in with your team. You hired for culture fit first, so that's the first thing you need to measure.

Ultimately, you want to know if your assumptions were correct, and you found someone that fits your team.

What you're doing here is making sure that they're acclimating well. If not, it's time to make some adjustments.

Take a good look at their first two weeks' performance and ask:

- Do you see promise for them?

- Do you see the potential you hired them for?

- Are they using the training you've provided?

- Are the conversations productive?

- Are they open to feedback?

- Are they open to giving *you* feedback?

On the subject of feedback, don't hesitate to ask your new employee for it. When you get the feedback, let them know what you plan to do to address their concerns. In this way, you can model the way you want to see everyone in the organization handle feedback. It's one more piece of culture that you enforce in these early days.

Four Weeks

During the first two weeks, you introduced your employee to their metrics. At the four-week mark, it is time to start holding them accountable to those metrics. By this stage of the 2:4:12 Launch, a new employee is acclimated to the process. They understand basic procedures. They know the team.

Some employees will graduate to this point earlier than others. Remember, the 2:4:12 Launch involves overlapping weeks. For those new hires who get through all their responsibilities for the first two weeks in a few days, they can move into their four-week period immediately. Others will be slower.

This process is driven by their own personal motivations and requirements.

For those slower employees, it's important to be understanding. Letting them go at this point is an expensive and time-consuming choice. Your new hires are meant to be long-term employees, and when your aim is years of high performance, a few extra weeks of onboarding won't amount to much.

Instead of expecting perfection at this point, you want to improve how your new people fit the team from a productivity, skills, and role perspective.

You can think of week four as your new hire's checkup. They aren't expected to be fully OTR[2] yet, but you want to see the progress. And just as crucially, you need them to communicate what they need to be a top performer.

Now start giving them more independence. You might give them tasks like checking in with their mentor after a full shift or getting on your calendar for a meeting. They should be able to handle that along with more responsibility in their actual work.

You'll provide less oversight here, but you also want to have a check-in meeting where you discuss unmet expectations—on both sides. Keep in mind that you are not admitting (or assigning) fault when expectations aren't yet met. At this stage, you are simply acknowledging that expectations are often not aligned. You want to get to that alignment as a team.

This will help you establish clear and consistent communication and provide room for feedback on all sides. During this stage of onboarding, it's common for new hires to question and identify processes that don't make sense. Be open to their feedback, and don't hesitate to give them feedback too.

Checking in at four weeks allows you to troubleshoot any issues before they become serious problems down the line. It opens the communication lines and makes clear you take an active role in the success of the company.

Here, you're setting the tone for your future relationship: one in which you expect your people to hit their metrics, but you're always ready to discuss what they need to better perform.

Questions to Ask at Four Weeks

A conversation at four weeks after starting is possibly one that your new hire has never had. It can feel awkward to be called into the boss's office after four weeks to talk about metrics and expectations on a twelve-week program. It's also rare that these encounters are real conversations—set up in a way to show partnership and allow the employee to take the lead.

For all those reasons, you need some icebreakers. Ask your new team member questions that facilitate an open, honest dialogue:

- How are you feeling after your first weeks?

- What has happened so far that you didn't expect?

- How well do you understand how your work is measured?

- Where are we missing the mark?

- What expectations weren't met?

- Why do you feel they haven't been met?

These check-ins are not a time to wing it. You're setting expectations for the entire future relationship you have with this person. Be prepared and make the time useful for everyone. Create a dialogue of constructive feedback. Take the opportunity to share any unmet expectations on your side. For example: *You said you could accomplish X, but I see it's been challenging for you. How can we work on that together?*

This is also an opportunity to discover problems in the hiring process you can fix before your next round of recruitment. For example, how do you tweak your interview process? Did you ask the right questions and set the right expectations? Did you have the right conversations?

Twelve Weeks

Once a new employee reaches twelve weeks with your company, they should be ready to take ownership of their role and their results. They know what is expected when it comes to their job and your company's culture. They are comfortable giving and receiving feedback and starting the conversation themselves.

Now they are ready to step up as you step away from oversight. You want to be in a position where they guide themselves because they are capable of following the process in their own unique way, setting their own goals, and taking ownership of their results. They know the culture, they know the metrics, and they've had twelve weeks to iron out misunderstandings. Now it's on them.

If they aren't ready to be independent in their position now, it's unlikely they will ever be. It's time to let them go and reassess your hiring process to make sure you didn't miss something before making them an offer.

From here forward, they'll be setting their own quarterly goals in alignment with the company's goals. Once they know where the company is going, they decide what they need to help the company move forward and meet its objectives.

This could be new training, a new process, or overcoming something that prevents them from performing their best.

Now comes the difficult part for business leaders: you have to trust your people. Their goals may not seem like the best objectives to you. Take this real-life example that one of our clients dealt with. Imagine if one of your new team members sets a goal of reorganizing their desk for the quarter.

On the surface, it may be difficult to understand how this is going to drive your employee forward or help you hit the company's goals. But you need to let them set it, or you risk them never taking ownership of their role and results. It is OK to ask how they see this helping the company's objectives. Just because you might question the goal doesn't mean that you overrule them on it. That employee may be struggling with organization. Cleaning up their desk may help them clean up their calendar or organize their notes from recent jobs. Only they know what they truly need to perform.

You can ask them to elaborate if you don't understand how their goals will lead them to take ownership of their results and role—but ultimately, you have to leave it to them.

If, after the quarter ends, their metrics haven't improved, then it's time to have another conversation.

"You've finished cleaning your desk, but you aren't more efficient. What do you need? What's a goal that could really push you forward next quarter?"

If this happens two or more times, you know that they are either in the wrong role and you need to find another place in the company for them, or they aren't aligned with the company's goals.

Instead of firing them on the spot, this is where the Core Fit Conversation (see the next chapter) can help. But you'll only find how you can help them if you ask and take in their response with an open mind.

Remember, accountability goes both ways.

Questions to Ask at Twelve Weeks

Zig Ziglar, renowned business leadership expert and motivational speaker, used to describe onboarding like priming a pump. Once the pump gets the water going, it flows steadily.

The first twelve weeks—the entire 2:4:12 Launch—is where you're priming the pump for your new hire. If you focus on setting up employees to win their first quarter, it's easier to keep them engaged long-term. Here are some questions to ask yourself:

- How well do they win in the job?

- How are they driving performance?

- How well are they setting goals?

- How do they compare to the rest of the team?

- How well do they know where the company is going?

- When they make a mistake, do they blame others or take responsibility?

- How well do they solve problems?

- How well are they learning and growing?

As you consider these questions, look to see how primed the pump is now for a flow of independent, dedicated success for years to come.

TAKE ACTION

Did you hire someone amazing who you are ready to onboard? Start by patting yourself on the back. Then share your excitement with the team and its newest member. Make a point to celebrate your new additions.

Set the new employee up to win in their new role. Pair them with an experienced worker who will be their mentor. Make sure they are supported to learn their job. Create and implement structures to infuse your Core into their day-to-day.

During the first two weeks of onboarding, set expectations and establish their metrics. Tell them you don't expect them to produce right away, but don't let that be an excuse for them to slack off.

At four weeks, check in with your new employee. Ask them how it's going. Talk about unmet expectations if there are any. Reset if needed.

After twelve weeks of an effective onboarding program, your employee will own their role and their results. If they are setting their own goals and can work autonomously to hit their numbers, onboarding was a success.

Checklist

- ☐ Celebrate new hires by introducing them to the team in a way that aligns with their personality type.

- ☐ Describe your expectations for the job they just started. Make it clear from the start your plan for the next twelve weeks.

- ☐ Explain that during the first two weeks, it's about getting acclimated and understanding the company culture. They'll be working but you're not holding them accountable to metrics yet.

- ☐ During the first four weeks, get them up to speed on how to perform in the role. Assign them a mentor who can help them speed up the process.

- ☐ At the four-week mark, meet with your new hire to review any unmet expectations on both sides. Adjust if needed.

- ☐ At the end of the twelve weeks, they should be ready to own their role and their results. Keep them on track to achieve these results.

- ☐ Be available to your new hire. When they have questions, make it easy for them to ask and get a timely response.

☐ If someone doesn't make it past the twelve weeks, assess your hiring process to see what you missed. Adjust as necessary.

7

ENGAGE

In my entire career as a team lead on a floor at Bank of America with over two hundred people, I only fired a handful of people. Everyone else that came to my team turned into a high performer. I learned early on that if you're willing to see workers as people, you can save a lot of time, money, and mental hardship for yourself and your team. When a worker isn't engaged, it's often a simple fix.

One of the people I'll never forget was Jackie. She was considered the worst performer on another team, and her manager transferred her to me. That first day we met, she came into my office crying.

"I'm getting fired, aren't I?" she asked.

"That's really up to you," I told her.

We spoke for three hours about her performance, what was expected of her, and what she understood about her role. I learned the problem was that her shift started at 8:00 a.m., but her two-year-old daughter's school opened at the exact same time. Jackie's old boss knew this but told her she needed to figure it out herself. So, she would get to work at 8:15 a.m., and her boss would grill her for being late to set an example for the rest of the team.

Jackie enjoyed her work, but she had a boss breathing down her neck who was inflexible.

During that conversation with Jackie, we completely reset expectations, and I changed Jackie's schedule. I told her she would start at 8:30 a.m. and work thirty minutes later instead.

Within a month, she became a top performer on the team. It was such a dramatic shift that her old boss accused me of cheating the system. But Jackie was the one who deserved the most credit—because she put in the extra effort. She got what she needed. She took on the extra work because she felt appreciated. The company invested in her, so she reinvested in it.

From that time, I learned a critical lesson: what you put in is what you get back.

—RYAN

Almost every worker has the potential to be a Jackie. People want to be seen and heard. They want someone to care and engage with them beyond just telling them what is expected from a performance perspective. They want to know they are valued—that their needs are being met and that you know they have a life outside of work.

Every person has massive potential, but you can only unlock that when you understand that every person is only human. They have drama at home. They have kids that aren't doing well in school. They have a sick spouse or elderly parents. Most employers know this, and yet some will easily fall into the mindset that an employee is only a set of hands.

But if you want your employees to care about the company, *you* have to care about the things that are important to *them*.

And to show that, you have to *engage* with them on a much deeper level.

Engagement is all about reinforcing your communication and leadership style. It's about integrating people deeply into your culture. And it's about unlocking the potential of people like Jackie, who you already have on your team.

This is a natural extension of the company you already presented to your new hires. During The Wait, you demonstrated that you cared. During Onboard, you shared with them how to belong, how to perform, and how to win. Now, you're simply reinforcing the behaviors and communication that you've already established.

The type of culture integration that needs to happen during Engage is not just about having employees learn a list of core values. It's about being intentional when reinforcing team standards and norms.

STAY ENGAGED

Engagement is, according to Forbes, "the emotional commitment the employee has to the organization and its goals"—and enhancing that commitment is perhaps the greatest tool you have to drive growth through your team. This isn't just about anecdotal evidence like Jackie's story. According to data by Gallup, highly engaged teams produce at 21 percent more profitability across industries, company size, location, and economic conditions.

Organizations and teams are nearly twice as likely to succeed when employee engagement scores reach the top quartile. This leads to a 41 percent reduction in absenteeism and 59 percent less turnover, along with a 17 percent increase in productivity and a 20 percent boost in sales.

Maintaining engagement, though, can be tricky. Imagine you have a Rock Star salesperson on your team. Every week, they're crushing it. But as time goes on, you see they start to lose some enthusiasm for the work. It's become too easy.

The usual solution here is to just promote them. From your perspective, that's a huge win. They can keep doing what they do so well, and they can coach up the rest of the team to the same level.

The only problem is that they don't want to be a manager. They'll take it—because who turns down more money and career advancement? But because management is outside their skillset, their engagement will plummet.

In other words, promotion is not always the best solution to maintain engagement. You need a better set of tools.

A TEAM MEMBER FIT FOR ENGAGEMENT

Before we get to the process of engaging your team, we should take a moment to be sure each new member is fit to progress any further.

At this point, you must be sure this person is ready to be engaged. After a rigorous interview and a thorough onboarding, you will know if this person is a good fit for your organization.

By now, when you follow this process, it will be clear whether a new hire fits your company culture or not. If they don't, it's important to let them go—for their benefit and yours. We've seen owners keep people long past the point of any mutual benefit. We get it. It's tough to let someone go after they've joined the team. We've been there too.

But as a leader, one of the best things you can do for yourself, your team, and the employee is to let them go find a position that meets their needs.

Jeff Weiner, CEO of LinkedIn, says this is one of the most important lessons he's learned as a leader. In an interview with CNBC, he said, "Do not leave the pitcher in the game for too long." As Weiner explains, keeping someone in the wrong role is one of the least compassionate things you can do. They need to move on and find a better fit, and so do you.

What you want at the engagement stage are employees who are excellent at their individual jobs and also excellent members of your team. They just fit.

Core Values in Action

Every group has cultural norms. They happen naturally. It's human nature. People conform to the behaviors that are common in a group. This is part of the value of engaging with new hires. This is your chance to be intentional about the behaviors and Core Values you model.

When we work with clients, it's often the case that every employee knows the company's Core Values...in theory. But it's crickets when we ask those same employees to explain how the Core Values are implemented in the workplace.

Leadership has a tendency to make team members memorize lists of values without knowing how to live those values. This is why you must embed your Core Values in everything you do— and then create a structure for integrating new people into your culture.

The engagement stage is a perfect chance to introduce your Core Values in action and reinforce them with your existing team. This is not the place to be "hands off" and hope that the right values manifest themselves. Nor is it the time to hand a new employee a one-page bullet list of every value the company holds. Instead, be proactive and show them how you want them to behave.

Ask yourself what your company does differently in some of the key components of its operations:

- How does your organization operate uniquely?

- How does communication work?

- How does the team make decisions?

- How does it live its Core Values?

As you display and reinforce your values and expectations with your new and seasoned employees, be sure to hold people accountable when they fall short. Call them out. Encourage your team to hold each other accountable too.

CREATING A BASELINE

Creating structures for engagement can feel overwhelming, but it doesn't have to be. We've had clients make a big deal out of a team member demonstrating Core Values. When they see someone exemplifying their values in a very clear way, it gets documented and celebrated. They share it on social media, in the company newsletter, and at the next team meeting.

To create additional structures for engagement, have regular conversations about your values. If continuous improvement is a Core Value of your company, you might ask your employees questions like:

- What would it be like if everyone lived with this mindset of continuous improvement?

- What would it be like if everyone continuously improved?

- How do you find yourself continuously improving in your life?

- If you were to look at the company, how would you know your boss is continuously improving?

When you evaluate the effectiveness of your structures for engagement, there is no universal standard that you have to meet. Instead, it's important to establish a baseline for your company or team and measure an employee's engagement relative to that base value. From there, you should aim to see progress—or, in the case of already exemplary employees, sustainable high performance.

At some point in time, an employee who has undergone successful onboarding and engagement phases will max out and be a 10, and they're going to continue to strive to be a 10. The more critical part of having this baseline is to ensure that you don't see employees falling back.

We've had some clients create a measurement system around a three-point scale to measure a value like continuous improvement. For example, a three could be someone who is always reading a new book or enrolling in a new class on their own. A two could be an employee who follows their boss's instructions to attend training or a webinar but shows no initiative themself. And a one could be an employee who dodges every opportunity for improvement, never wanting to better themself.

By using this scale, they know who needs more engagement to move up the scale and embrace that Core Value.

As with every system in this book, when you're scoring values you want to be up front and intentional about what you're looking for. How are you scoring them? Is it a three-point system, a five-point system? Once you settle on a metric, remain consistent.

Getting someone new acclimated to your company culture—and raising up those disengaged and neutral team members—takes time, intentionality, and repetition. It takes a consistent measurement so they know where they stand and when they improve.

And it takes one-on-one conversations that dig into that Core.

THE CORE FIT CONVERSATION

One of the biggest predictors of high retention rates is how often you have quality one-on-one conversations with your team members. As reported in *Harvard Business Review*, "People who get twice the number of one-on-one meetings with their manager relative to their peers are 67 percent more likely to be engaged."

That doesn't mean any old interaction will do. You've brought in a team of high performers, and you want to reach out to them in a way that inspires and motivates them. For that, you need the Core Fit Conversation.

There are two types of conversations in this process. The first one happens at the end of an employee's first ninety days—after they complete the 2-4-12 Launch. The second conversation happens on a regular basis after that.

Everybody has their own spin on the Core Fit Conversation. There's no one right way to do it. Some companies have conversations that are very metrics driven. Some are very culture driven. And some are focused on communication. The only way you can really do this wrong is by not having Core Fit Conversations at all.

What Is a Core Fit Conversation?

Before we dig into the two types of Core Fit Conversations, let's first take a moment to define exactly what these are. As mentioned above, there's a lot of flexibility in this process, but that doesn't mean anything goes.

For instance, a Core Fit Conversation is not an engagement survey. That's not to say there's anything wrong with doing such surveys. Gallup, an American business analytics advisory, has a twelve-question survey that a lot of companies use to assess the effectiveness of their structures of engagement. There's real value in such products, but that's not what we're aiming to discuss in the Core Fit Conversation.

These are also not employee reviews where a boss tells a team member what they need to do better. Communication that is limited to top-down, "shut up and do as I say," is not what you, your employees, or the company needs.

The Core Fit Conversation is different. The aim is to establish a communication channel that is top-down *and* bottom-up—a true back-and-forth between the employee and their direct supervisor. Core Fit Conversations provide a process for effective dialogue across the company, and the means to keep that dialogue going.

Think about it like this: in any relationship, there comes a point at which you need to discuss whether this will be a long-term thing. Are you planning to stay together, or is one of you ready to move on?

For business leaders and employees, ninety days is a natural time to sit down, talk through what's going on, and discuss where this relationship is going. Are both of you interested in seeing this relationship move forward together? And if you both are, what should that relationship look like?

This is how you find, empower, and sustain Jackies across your company. It's also how you take unengaged employees and turn them into a motivated, dedicated team that will push for the best results for years to come.

The First Core Fit Conversation

The first Core Fit Conversation happens when the 2-4-12 Launch ends. This conversation should take place between the employee and their direct supervisor. However, that doesn't have to be the case. This could be between someone in HR if it makes everyone more comfortable—although if open and honest communication is an issue by now, you'll want to address that quickly.

During that first Core Fit Conversation, you should answer these questions:

- What did you learn about your new employee during the onboarding process?

- Did the onboarding process succeed in accomplishing its goals?

- What can you do to improve the process?

Crucially, this is not the stage to evaluate fit. A bad hire should *not* have lasted this long in the hiring and onboarding process. Throughout the screening process, interviews, and onboarding you should be fully committed to the person sitting in front of you.

You can be confident this is the right team member for this position.

For this first Core Fit Conversation, your aim is to have a dialogue about the relationship's future. Start by looking at your own process and seeing where you can improve. This shows that you're open to feedback and that this conversation is unlike those employee reviews your team member has experienced at other companies.

You might consider asking questions like these:

- How would you rate your overall onboarding process from 1 to 10? Using one word, what would make it a 10?

- How well have your expectations been met from 1 to 10? What would make it a 10?

- How well do you feel you and your supervisor get along?

- What support have you received since you started that worked or didn't work?

- What do you feel I need to start, or stop, doing?

- How would you rate your overall performance here?

- Do you fully understand how your performance is being measured?

- What would you say to a friend or family member considering joining our team?

- How well do you feel we're making decisions that align with our vision, values, and purpose?

- How transparent do you feel you can be?

- What can we do to improve our recruiting process?

From there, you can turn to your employee's performance. But again, don't lecture. Instead, ask them what they think about how they're doing. Get them to think critically. Ask a simple question like, "What is one thing you think you could start doing to improve your performance?" A question like that further entrenches that spirit of independence you want from your team, and it shows you truly do have faith in them to be responsible for their own performance.

It might take some time to work through these questions, but everyone needs this time. We recommend no less than one hour for this conversation. This is a moment in which a real mindset shift can happen for your new employee. It's proof that even once the hiring process is over, you still stand by those values you've been sharing with them from the start.

And it's an opportunity for you to get some valuable feedback. There's potential for some new ideas from the people who have gone through your Core Fit Hiring process. But it's also a chance to see proof that this system really works. It's validation of everything you've done so far.

The Core Fit Conversation Checkup

After the first Core Fit Conversation, you want to have regular conversations with each employee. The timing for these conversations depends on your company and the value you gain from getting this feedback from your team. These sessions must be something that everyone looks forward to—not something that people are tired of or unprepared for. They can happen once a year, once a quarter, or even once a month.

We usually advise clients to shoot for once per quarter with every employee, regardless of their position. That's often enough to maintain contact without being cumbersome to anyone involved.

The value of these regular meetings is that you keep up with their world as it changes. Yes, by now, you've set each employee on a path for success, fulfillment, and excellence. Of course, life changes. Priorities shift, goals evolve, and systems become outdated.

Remember, your employees are people with great potential, not just a pair of hands. Each one of them is a potential Jackie for your organization. And you want to make sure you are always doing what you can to allow them to reach that potential.

While they may be aligned and fulfilled in their role immediately after the 2-4-12 Launch, their performance and engagement will change as the company and leadership change. A role that fits them today may not in a year.

You may have seen promising employees start off as top performers only to get bored, become less engaged, and start seeking new opportunities elsewhere within a few quarters. They go from engaged to neutral to disengaged to gone before your eyes.

It's possible that they changed personally, and they are no longer aligned to your Core. It's possible the business itself shifted directions and the needs of the business shifted with it. It's possible personal circumstances are making it hard to give everything they have to your organization.

You might be able to do something about all these issues, but you can only do that if you know what's happening. And that requires an honest conversation.

The Core Fit Conversation is about maintaining the back-and-forth chain of communication to identify areas for improvement on both sides. The quarterly Core Fit Conversation is about maintenance, problem-solving, and identifying major issues *before* they happen.

During this dialogue, you might ask questions like:

- How well is the employee still aligned to our Core?

- How well are you—the employer—and the company behaving consistently to your Core?

- What do you need from the employee that you aren't currently getting?

- What does the employee need from you and the team that they aren't getting?

- Where are they in relation to their professional goals?

- Where are they in relation to their personal goals?

- How is their personal life affecting their work performance?

Many of our clients ask questions like these and rate employees on a scale of red, yellow, and green. If an answer is in the red, there is a problem that should be addressed immediately. If it's yellow, there are concerns that need to be looked at or monitored. A green evaluation means everything is going as expected.

When you and your employees are in the habit of communication and assessment, you are able to address issues as things change. You'll know when the company isn't living up to its Core Values or when an employee's role no longer fits.

Instead of putting out fires as crises arise, you can seize an opportunity before it becomes a problem. For example, one employee may want to improve a certain skill, but their role doesn't allow for the growth they want. Maybe they want to be a mentor for new employees, but they are always quietly working on job sites alone.

Left unattended, that engaged employee drifts toward disengagement and may start looking for a company that offers them more. But after a conversation with you, they could become a true team leader.

Your regular Core Fit Conversation can allow you to identify when an employee no longer fits a particular role (or even the whole company) anymore. It allows you to ensure that everyone finds their *best* fit in their role. This is as true for your engaged A players as for the disengaged C players you want to turn around.

And the only way to adjust fit is to stay engaged through these conversations.

GROWTH ACCELERATOR PROGRAM

There's another valuable use of your Core Fit Conversations. You can use them to find out where each employee is in relation to their own goals.

A Growth Accelerator Program, or GAP, is an employee-led personal and professional development program in which every quarter, a worker picks a goal or project to work on personally. It helps each employee fill the GAP between where they are and where they want to be.

Most companies offer professional development programs because that helps the business. GAP is different. It lets employees determine what they need for their professional and personal development.

This isn't just the right thing to do, it's a powerful tool for retention. Any personal growth a company pays for will net a massive return on investment. Your business will experience higher retention, greater performance, and happier, more productive employees.

Your employees will love GAP because it makes them feel appreciated. And employees who feel appreciated work harder and stick around longer.

To really increase the engagement of your Growth Accelerator Program, do it in conjunction with the Core Fit Conversation. Part of the beauty of this program is that it doesn't require much from you. As a leader, you don't have to worry about managing things. Your only responsibility is creating a list of approved programs and asking your employees to select their goals for the quarter. Beyond that, it is on each person to select the right program and hold themself accountable.

Here's what the engagement level can look like over time when you implement the principles we're sharing in this chapter.

EMPLOYEE ENGAGEMENT LEVEL

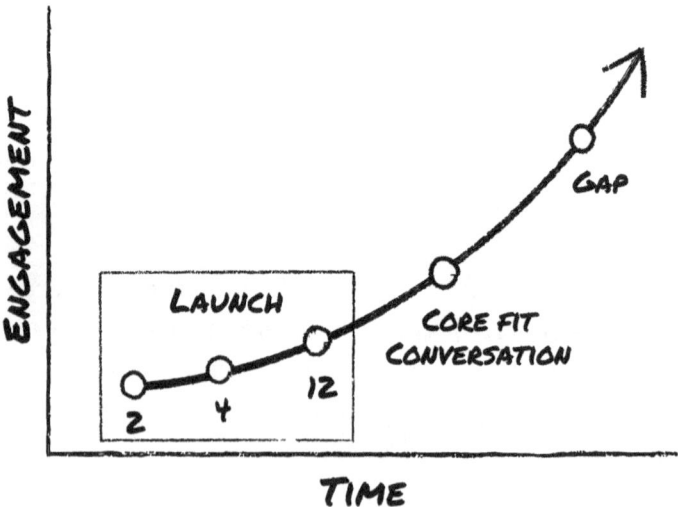

ENGAGEMENT

LAUNCH

GAP

CORE FIT
CONVERSATION

2 4 12

TIME

That said, you do want to put some parameters in place. It could be valuable to create a system in which workers collaborate with a mentor or manager to set their goals. You'll also want to focus on transferable skills that employees can use at home or in their roles. There also needs to be monitoring in place to mark progress.

A GAP offering can be as simple as offering foreign language support. We have clients with a large number of Spanish-speaking workers. So, the company pays for team members to learn Spanish or English. Another popular program is financial management. Something we often hear from employers is that many of their employees live paycheck to paycheck—some struggle to stretch each check that far. It's not that they don't make enough money, they just struggle to live within their means because no one ever taught them how. For those team members, money management training can go a lot further than a raise.

These sorts of skills can help your people throughout their lives. And if training like this is available every quarter, who would want to leave a company that offers that?

The Three-Year Plan

If you're so inclined, you can push the value of GAP even further. Instead of creating a customized development for each team member, you can create a three-year growth accelerator. This is basically a three-year personal and professional growth plan with some customizable components for employees.

Inside this specific growth accelerator model are twelve quarters of personal and professional development across a three-year period.

Year one is all about investing in the person culturally. How does an employee become a better leader and a better communicator? How can they better fit within the company?

In year two, look toward personal development. What can you do to help them grow and develop personally? This is where that money management course might come in. In some cases, you could even encourage your employees to bring their partner along to do training with them.

You can also include online training where employees can choose their own skills development. This would be a perfect opportunity for one of your employees who has always wanted to learn how to use Excel to finally do so. Such training is low cost and may allow that worker to eventually move into a leadership position.

This would blend nicely into the final year of the three-year Growth Accelerator Program, which is focused on career trajectory and long-term planning.

The program here must offer multiple paths. Some Superstar employees really want to push themselves forward and develop skills to advance in the company. But your Rock Stars are more likely to want to get a bit better at their craft. Maybe they want to get a certification, or maybe they want to take on a different kind of project. You can use the Core Fit Conversation to help direct each person down the best path for them.

Of course, you don't have to follow this three-year plan exactly. This could be a four-year plan—or even more. It's all about having a framework for consistency that is still customizable to the needs of your employees.

Once you have a program like this in place, you'll have happier and more productive people for your company. They'll want to stick around across that yearslong program—and if that changes, you'll know within the quarter thanks to your Core Fit Conversation.

Studies have shown that companies that invest in the personal growth of their people have higher retention rates over five years. Most workers today will sacrifice higher pay for a company that invests in their development. According to statistics gathered by the Lorman Team, "approximately 70 percent of employees would be somewhat likely to leave their current job to work for an organization known for investing in employee development and learning." What's shocking is that the percentage isn't higher. Who doesn't want to work for an employer who betters their lives?

And who wouldn't recommend such a place to their friends and family? With programs like these in place, your people will be more likely to refer high-quality employees to you down the line. Now, they have a compelling reason why their friends should apply to work for you. No one else is going to offer this kind of engagement and a program that opens up so many opportunities.

More retention, better applicants, and a team constantly improving its skills. Now that is a recipe for better results for far less work on your part.

TAKE ACTION

Engage new employees immediately and get them started on the right track with the Core Fit Conversation and a Growth Accelerator Program.

Both will be unique to your business, so involve your team in developing them. Don't overthink these processes. This is one of those areas in the Core Fit Hiring System where "done is better than perfect." As you roll these out, you'll get the feedback you need to improve the results of each and make them a critical process for engaging your employees.

Checklist

☐ Schedule a Core Fit Conversation with one of your direct reports to take place in the next month. Don't worry about what you'll discuss. Instead, focus on the habit of meeting with your people on a regular basis.

☐ After your first Core Fit Conversation, write down a series of questions to ask for future conversations. Focus on the feedback you get from your team that will help you be a better leader and provide a more engaging workplace.

☐ What will you offer for your Growth Accelerator Program? Ask your team what they want! Then create a program to give them what they need.

8

ASSESS

There's nothing more frustrating than a no-call, no-show for interviews, and we were getting very frustrated. We kept setting up interviews that no one ever attended. That's when we contacted Ryan and Jeremy.

They came in with two key questions: "How long is it taking you to call candidates after they apply? And how long does it take after that call for a branch manager to reach out with their interview schedule?"

Digging through our data, we discovered two things. First, the answer to that second question was far longer than we thought. On average, it was taking four days for a branch manager to meet with the candidate after our initial call.

We were filling entry-level positions, so those applicants had new jobs by then.

To improve the process, we told the branch managers they had to respond within twenty-four hours after we had the first call.

The second discovery wasn't from data but from assessing technique. Christine made all the calls to the applicants. Listening to her calls, we found out she sounded robotic. She asked the same questions every time in a dull tone of voice. There was no enthusiasm. Even when the applicant volunteered information to personalize the conversation, she'd ignore it and just move on.

After this realization, we pulled Christine aside and got her some coaching, teaching her how to vary and personalize the conversation.

This was all information we'd had for months. But it was only when we realized we should assess it that these revelations came to light.

Once we acted on that information, though, we flipped our numbers. We went from a 90 percent ghosting rate to a 90 percent show-up rate in less than a month. We went from as bad as you can get to as good as you can get.

—TOM, HR manager in a Virginia home services company

At this point, you have new hires who have been onboarded and integrated into your team. You have a system to regularly engage with them. And all of this aligns with your Core. What's left to cover?

With the Core Fit Hiring System, your hiring process is certain to bring in better applicants who become better candidates and who evolve into better employees. But any process can improve. So, if you want to keep hiring better people faster, you need to evaluate your hiring system often to maintain its effectiveness. And when you evaluate, you need concrete ways to grade performance. You need to be able to watch your numbers, review your metrics, and track and tweak systems for each component of the Core Fit Hiring System—otherwise, you end up in Tom's position, making guesses about where there is value in the process.

It's important to note that this is not a supplemental step. The risk of implementing this system without the Assess component can't be overestimated. If you don't track progress and make tweaks over time, you will end up right back where you were at the start of this book. On the flip side, you don't want to make changes just to make changes. You want to make changes that are relevant, that are going to get you results, or that will move your company in the right direction.

At the same time, assessing is by its nature more technical. All the information ahead is important. However, you will want to take your time reading, processing, and implementing this.

Assessing begins with identifying metrics for success. Once you measure the distance between your goals and your results, you can implement the necessary change within your system to reach ever greater heights.

SETTING YOUR METRICS

In previous chapters, we talked about how to assess the employees you recruit. In this chapter, you'll discover how to assess and troubleshoot the recruiting system itself. And that starts with establishing metrics.

Peter Drucker said, "What gets measured, gets managed." Recruiting is no different. You must measure the work you're putting in against the results you're getting back.

Those metrics should include:

- Number of new applicants

- Percentage of new candidates

- Number of hires per source

- Pipeline conversion rate

- Number of days in pipeline

- Time to first contact

- Time to hire (in days)

- Number of offers made/accepted

- Cost per hire

- Turnover

Your ATS should allow you to track these metrics. Together, these metrics give you a picture of what is working and what needs improvement to continue to drive the best talent to your team.

Number of New Applications

This is the total number of new applications you receive across all your recruitment platforms. By new, we mean first-time applicants who have seen your job ad and clicked on it at one source or another.

The number of new applications shows you how effective your ads are at attracting applicants from your target market. If you're not getting enough new applications, you must ask yourself why. It could be that your ads aren't performing well. Maybe they're not keyword optimized. Maybe the job titles are too creative and don't make sense.

Percentage of New Candidates

Getting a ton of new applicants is promising—but it's really only valuable if a sizable number of those applicants become candidates. As a reminder, an applicant is someone who applies, while a candidate is someone qualified that you want to talk to. In other words, applicants assess quantity while candidates assess quality.

As with other metrics, you want to monitor the trend: is the percentage going up, staying the same, or going down? If the percentage goes down, you have a few questions to consider:

- Are your screening questions too difficult or irrelevant?

- Are you letting the ATS screen people for you?

- Is there something in your ad attracting the wrong people?

Number of Hires per Source

If the number of applications is trending down across multiple sources, that may suggest there's a problem with the content you're putting there. It may be time to return to the 360 Marketing Plan, the Core Fit Profile, and your job ads.

If the downward trend is only at a single source, ask yourself, "Why?" Maybe there's been a rule change to how job listings can be posted on the platform, and now your ads are getting delisted.

Once you've explored the situation, if it seems to be the platform that's the problem, it may be time to allocate your resources elsewhere.

Applications per Hire

How many applications do you need to make one hire? This may change based on the position, but an average tells you what's happening. Let's say you know you need 117 applications, on average, to get one new hire. If you were getting fewer than 117 applications for a position, you know you're less likely to find that ideal hire.

You can also use this number as a benchmark. If you go through more than your average number of applications per new hire during the next hiring cycle, there may be a potential issue with the interview process and how you're screening people. Perhaps there's a hiring manager who isn't following the process. Without this number, you may never know.

Pipeline Conversion Rates

Your pipeline runs from applicant to candidate to hire. This metric tells you what percentage of people are transitioning to the later stages of the process. For that reason, this is actually two metrics in one:

- Percentage of applicants converting to candidates

- Percentage of candidates converting to new hires

For example, you might have your job posted on a Monday and get two hundred applications by Friday. In the second week, you might only get thirty new applications. While the number of applications might fluctuate weekly, your pipeline conversion rate shouldn't change. You should have the same percentage of applicants becoming candidates and the same percentage of candidates who become new hires. If those percentages drop, once again, you know something in the process needs repair.

Number of Days in Pipeline

It takes, on average, thirty days for someone to make a new hire from the time the applicant enters the pipeline. The target number of days we like to see for most clients is two weeks in the pipeline before the decision is made on whether or not to hire the candidate.

Unlike some of the other metrics here, this is not one you necessarily want to improve upon. Consistency is more important here than constant improvement. We know there are hiring managers who would love to lower that target number below two weeks. When that perfect candidate walks in the door, they want to hire them on the spot. But one of the lessons of this book is that such hiring practices often lead to problems down the line—the very sort of problems that brought you here.

What you want from this number, then, is steadiness. If you're recognizing talent within two weeks and moving them forward in the hiring process, your system is doing its job.

Time to First Contact (In Hours)

According to CareerPlug, the average time to first contact a new applicant is 7.93 days. The target number we like to give clients for time to first contact is fifteen minutes.

Yes, you read that correctly. Fifteen minutes.

This is how soon you want to make the personal outreach covered in Automate once the application has been reviewed. You want to make this personal connection as quickly as possible once you know the applicant meets the basic parameters for the job. For the top talent, the canned, "We received your application" email is not going to be enough. The message has to be personal, and it has to come fast.

To be fair, someone is rarely able to consistently hit fifteen minutes to first contact. Time to first contact is a number you want to be as low as possible. If this number is going up suddenly, and it's taking longer to establish your first contact with a candidate, you have a process issue.

Number of Offers Made/Accepted

Across industries, on average, two out of three offers are accepted. A lower number could indicate that your candidates and positions are not a good match, which means there's an issue with one of the key components earlier in the hiring system.

In some cases, a higher or lower rate of acceptance is reflective of the competitiveness or specialization of the industry or position itself and may not indicate something is wrong with your hiring system. For instance, for entry-level positions, the rate of acceptance is often lower. It could also be impacted when taking too long to make the offer or follow up on it as job seekers often have to move quickly to find a new job.

Cost per Application/Cost per Hire

How much money are you spending on the job boards and advertising to drive one application? How much does it cost you to hire one person?

Much like time to hire, the cost per application and the cost per hire often move in the same direction. In both cases, you must consider opportunity costs, including time taken away from other projects. If you had a hiring manager interviewing candidates for your HR team, for example, they're no longer managing for that hour and a half.

While you're not writing checks for every cost, it's important to track the resources that go into a successful hire, from time to energy to dollar amounts.

Unlike some of the other earlier components, a high or low cost here is not a definitive indicator of success or failure in your hiring system. In fact, we had one client who calculated the cost per bad hire to be $66,000. You can bet they were going to get it right and find the perfect new team member for their team. For them, $66,000 was a high number, but not necessarily a "wrong" number. Not every company spends that much on hires, but the number is often higher than you think. The national average for an entry-level position is $4,906 when considering everything that goes into it.

You want to find what are the "right" numbers for your company here, and then track progress from there.

Turnover

All this effort to hire is only worth it if your employees stick around for a while. For that reason, you need to track retention. We always look at turnover as it relates to the number of people you've hired.

Here's the formula:

1. Number of new hires terminated in the first ninety days / number of people hired in the last ninety days

2. Number of people terminated who were employed longer than ninety days / number of employees in the same time frame

These numbers can be illuminating. When business leaders come to us, they often think they have a recruiting problem. After we look at these metrics, we often find that the problem isn't hiring people, it's keeping them.

Here's the basic rule of thumb. If someone terminates in the first ninety days of employment, you have a recruiting issue. If it's longer than ninety days, you have a culture, leadership, or communication problem. It's important you know which one is affecting your turnover so you can solve it correctly.

ASSESSING THE CORE FIT HIRING SYSTEM

Once you have your key metrics in mind, you can begin assessing the system. Remember that assessing is a continual process that reveals inefficiencies or validates things are still working as expected.

When you evaluate your system, determine which areas could generate additional results and which ones are working at an optimal level. For example, reducing the cost per hire by decreasing the time to contact could have a dramatic impact on other areas of your business. Without continually assessing your processes, you would never know what's possible.

Using the Core Fit Hiring System as our model for assessment, here are a few questions you should ask before implementing changes.

Core

Questions to Evaluate Success

- Is your message still relevant?

- Is the job market stable? If not, what changes do you need to prepare for?

- Is your message still correct?

- Is your message still consistent?

- Does your team still get excited about your vision, purpose, and Core Values?

Implementing Changes

When you implement changes at the Core, you want these changes to improve the relevancy, consistency, and/or accuracy of your company's messaging.

Relevancy refers to what is important to your target market. What are applicants focused on? What are candidates' needs?

What do you need to change to increase alignment with those needs?

Consistency is about the presentation of information. What will people find when they research you? Is your logo the same on your website, social profiles, and careers page? What about your company messaging? Branding is not just about being out there. It's also about spreading a uniform message.

Accuracy touches on the quality of information about your company. After all, you could be consistently inaccurate about your brand messaging. So, does your Core accurately reflect your values, vision, purpose, and story? If not, what changes could bring the language you are using closer to your true Core?

All three of these components can require refinement over time.

One of the easiest ways to assess and improve the success of your Core is to listen to the feedback of your current employees. Show them your website and ask them, "Based on what you see here, would you want to work for us as a new hire? How relevant, consistent, and accurate is it to our company?"

Your Core message must really speak to the heart of your employees. Therefore, allow those who exemplify your Core to assess it regularly and suggest how relevant, consistent, and accurate it remains.

Find

Questions to Evaluate Success

- Are you advertising in the right places?

- Are you telling enough people?

- Are you targeting the right job seekers?

- Do you know where that job seeker is?

- Do you have a job ad that speaks to that job seeker?

Implementing Changes

The Find questions touch upon some of the deeper, more intrinsic possible issues with your Core Fit Profile. This is why Find is linked with Core. If your Core Values aren't alive and well, you'll have a tough time finding great employees who believe in and adhere to them.

While we don't have the time to go over every possible trend you'll see in your system's hiring data, we can go through a few common scenarios.

- **When you find limited prospects for hiring.** If you're seeing an insufficient quality of applications, chances are something's wrong with the scope of your

360 Marketing Plan. Review your Core Fit Profile and ensure that your plan is consistent with your Core.

- **When your ads aren't producing, even though you and your people think they're awesome.** You're likely looking for new hires in the wrong places. If your Core is relevant, consistent, and accurate (according to your current team), you must change where your ads display.

- **When you're caught off guard or surprised by anything that happens during the offer meeting.** If you're making offers to strong candidates and they're not accepting, it means the screening process does not reflect your Core Fit Profile, or you're not making a decision quickly enough.

Automate

Questions to Evaluate Success

- Have you built your recruiting funnel?

- Have you built your bench?

- Is your bench growing every month?

- Are you receiving enough applications to fill demand?

- Are you contacting people often enough?

- Has the quality of applicants changed?

- Are your hiring managers using the ATS?

- Is HR using the ATS to its full extent?

- Does your team trust the process?

- Are they able to use the ATS system the way the system was meant to be used?

Implementing Changes

In Automate, metrics should evaluate how well you adopt your ATS. When implementing changes for the Core Fit Hiring System, adoption is key—especially for Automate.

There are a few key components that directly reflect the success or failure of Automate, such as the time to first contact, time to fill, and time to hire. Sometimes, an ATS will also track that initial direct contact you make personally with the applicant. These are metrics directly related to the adoption of your ATS. Often when these numbers are moving in the wrong direction, it's because a part of your organization simply isn't using the system fully.

For this reason, implementing change in Automate is mostly about increasing the adoption rate of your ATS. There's often significant resistance here. Some see automation as taking control away from your team. Others struggle to learn new skills and technology when framed as "extra work" instead of "a necessary skill."

That's why, when you assess your automation process, you must ask yourself: does your team trust the process?

Because distrust leads to resistance, and resistance leads to work-arounds that lower the success of the process.

One of our clients had installed an ATS a year and a half before we started working with him. When we asked him to describe his process, he told us his team would get the applications into the ATS. And then, they would copy their information into an Excel spreadsheet and run everything out of it. When they contacted applicants, they wrote the emails themselves.

We had to double back on some of these details. Was this company really running everything through Excel instead of their ATS?

The client confirmed it. And worst of all, he didn't see anything wrong with that system.

It was a strange conversation to have because what his team was doing manually was exactly what the ATS was designed to do. He couldn't automate successfully because he didn't treat the ATS as a functional tool.

Before moving on, it's important to keep in mind with this step that things can break. Resistance to implementation may be the most common problem, but right behind it is an issue with the technology itself. The last thing you want to do is call your tech guy two weeks after a problem has surfaced, asking why you haven't been receiving any applications.

Automate is where you're going to see things break, so you need to be clear on the key metrics you will continually assess to make sure it is always working. In other words, assess its function as much as your team's behavior.

Interview

Questions to Evaluate Success

- Are candidates ghosting you?

- Are your interviews impactful enough?

- Are you scheduling the interview fast enough?

- Are you meeting with candidates frequently enough?

- Are you scoring candidates?

- Do the hiring managers, HR, and senior management follow the hiring process?

Implementing Changes

Implementing interview changes will require a bit of trial and error. Once you've hit the Interview phase, you're out of the technical and into the emotional and cultural aspects of the hiring process. It's no longer a numbers game you can easily check through metrics.

That's not to say metrics have no place. They will still be your guide, but there may be more to the story. You may find, for example, you're consistently seeing a low acceptance of offers. Instead of two out of three people taking your offer, you're closer to one in three. There can be several reasons why this happens. Sometimes, the problem traces all the way back to misaligned Core Values. But one of the most common issues is that candidates don't feel connected enough to your company. They like your company well enough, but they don't feel emotionally invested. They don't have enough skin in the game. And because they don't care, it's easier to take someone else's offer.

Consider what questions you're asking during the interview process. What comments are you making to the candidate's responses? How does your interview process express the excitement you feel just from having the opportunity to talk to them? People are more excited to talk when others seem excited to listen, and candidates will feel much more invested in working for your company if it seems like, from the beginning, you are invested in hiring them.

Consider if you're giving enough time for each candidate's interview. If fifteen minutes is not enough time to have a good conversation, then shoot for thirty minutes per interview. If thirty minutes is only enough to have a good but still shallow conversation, then shoot for sixty. "Enough" time is as much about establishing the important connection between the candidates and the company as it is in qualifying the candidate for the position.

Onboard

Questions to Evaluate Success

- Are employees excited and engaged on their first day of work?

- Are new employees acclimating well to the culture?

- Are new employees productive within the first four weeks?

- Is your existing team accepting new employees?

- Are people graduating to the launch of OTR[2]?

Implementing Changes

Problems at onboarding can sometimes be the most frustrating. After all the effort you've put in, it's extremely disheartening when those brilliant new hires struggle to step into the position. For that reason, it's all the more important to regularly assess this part of the process.

Make sure you are having an open and honest dialogue with the new team member and both of you are free to speak candidly about what is working and not working. Most of the changes you'll need to implement will focus on extending that means of communication.

While you strive to establish metrics and clear expectations here, remember that people and the company will change. What people need and how the company can best provide will transform over time. This is why consistent communication is so important. Be open to feedback and the potential for unmet expectations. Reset and reevaluate when needed.

You can back these conversations up with data by measuring the number of people to make it to ninety days and the number of people to hit OTR^2 targets.

Engage

Questions to Evaluate Success

- Are you integrating new and established hires into the company?

- Are your employees invested in their personal growth?

- Does the company provide employees with options to meet their growth goals?

- Do you have conversations with your employees about their values and expectations?

Implementing Changes

One of the most obvious problems encountered when assessing Engage is that employees don't stay engaged after the initial excitement as a new hire wears off. If you want your people engaged, then you must remain engaged with them.

If employees aren't staying engaged in the company's Core Vision, this may result from a lack of consistent individual attention. Are you regularly having conversations with the members of your team about your Core Vision and how it applies to them?

You may also find that your people don't feel the company is meeting their personal ambitions. According to a Harris Poll, 50 percent of employees don't know how they affect the company's goals. Have you helped them connect to the vision? Are there programs or training that your employees feel are missing or misaligned? Make sure they know what is available to them by communicating it regularly.

And once again, build those channels of communication to make sure feedback is getting to those who can make adjustments to this program.

TAKE ACTION

Assessment and adjustment are important for any system. If you put a process in place once and never evolve from there, you'll produce limited results and get diminishing returns.

Track the metrics you need to have a clear understanding of what is working in your Core Fit Hiring System and what could be improved. Connect that data to the various steps in your hiring process and make thoughtful changes to see improved results.

Even small changes can create greater success down the line.

Checklist

☐ Revisit the reporting available in your ATS and make sure that you're tracking the things that really matter. Put together a plan for how you'll watch these metrics each week so you know how to make better changes in your process.

☐ As your metrics move, look for trends and then identify the component of the Core Fit Hiring System that affects those results. Evaluate the changes you need to make.

☐ Revisit the process at least quarterly to make sure you're staying ahead of market changes and your team is still aligned with your hiring goals.

CONCLUSION

RECENTLY, WE HAD A CALL WITH A BUSINESS OWNER who used to have eight technicians in the field. He was meeting with us because that number had fallen to three recently. He was understandably upset. During the call, he talked about how horrible the job market was. As far as he was concerned, the sky was falling. He could think of a million reasons for his dilemma, but the one that never occurred to him was his hiring system.

Despite that lengthy conversation, we ultimately chose not to take him on as a client. There was simply little we could do for someone who wasn't willing to take control of their own company and make the changes necessary.

We can confidently predict you are a different kind of business owner. You picked up this book. You've read some tough truths and discovered the true hiring potential of your organization. And now, you've made it through the entire Core Fit Hiring System.

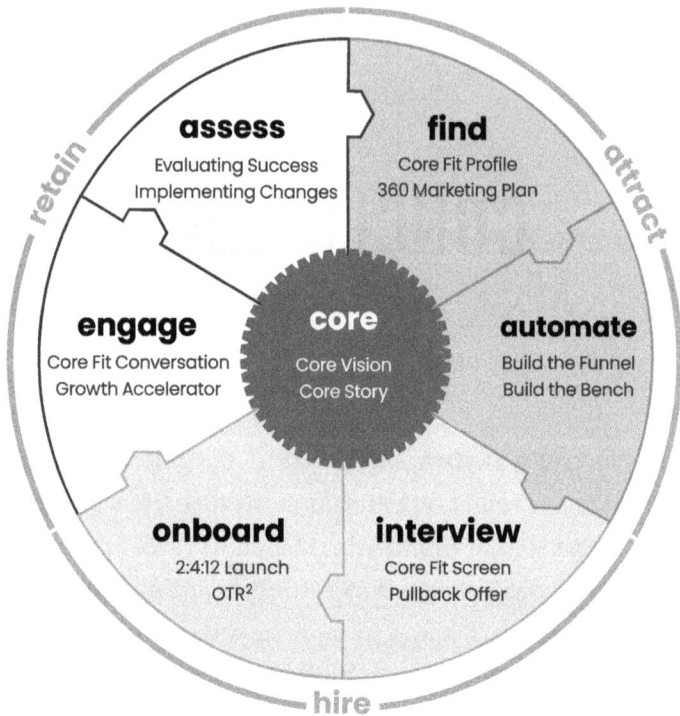

You may have started reading this book because you wanted to *hire better people faster*. Or maybe you wanted to be able to hire people, period. That's why most people would pick up a book like this, and that's usually the only goal people have when they start reading: *I want to hire more people.*

But you've come with us on a journey that has proven how much better hiring can unlock your organization. This system will allow you to hire more engaged, more qualified, and more invested employees. And those types of workers are far more productive and far more profitable. That means you can grow more successfully. It means you'll struggle less to achieve your business goals.

But it also means you can reclaim your life. You can enjoy time with your family, rediscover old hobbies, and think about life outside of work again. At the same time, your people will be better equipped for the challenges ahead and more fulfilled in their work. They'll know this company cares about them, and they'll show their appreciation by putting in that extra effort and staying in that position longer.

All that's left to do is to get started implementing this process.

Deciding where to start requires some self-assessment. In particular, you must answer one key question:

Where do you feel the most pain?

And that is where you start. Most of our clients come to us with a specific pain point. That's likely also true for you. You will eventually work around the entire model, but for now, figure out what is holding you back the most.

- Is the lack of high-quality hires holding you back from achieving your goals?

- Are you attracting enough high-quality applicants?

- Do you have great people interviewing, but your best candidates keep turning down a position?

- Are new hires ghosting you during onboarding?

- Are your new employees as engaged as the ones who have been with you for a while?

Answer that, and you have your starting point. Implementing the Core Fit Hiring System is a twofold process. You need to fix what's most broken first while simultaneously building every other component. Look at your biggest problem area. Go there. Focus on that while you continue developing each component carefully—your Core, Find, Automate, Interview, Onboard, Engage, and Assess.

By the end, with the right mindset and a continuous approach, you'll be hiring the top talent in your area. The business will be thriving. And you'll be sleeping better at night.

As you begin to improve your hiring process, remember: you'll make bad decisions. And as you learned in Assess, you'll never implement a perfect system. If you want to hire better people faster, you have to take responsibility for the quality of people applying for your jobs and the quality of people you're hiring.

Empower yourself as the agent of change in your own company. Instead of asking, "What's the problem?," turn it inward. "What can I do to remove this problem?"

In the beginning, take a bit of a personal journey and ask yourself tough, honest questions:

- Maybe none of your employees exemplify your company's Core. What can *you* do to improve the relevancy, consistency, and accuracy of your Core?

- Maybe the right people aren't applying. What can *you* do to find the target markets that will bring in the best applications for the job?

- Maybe you have a ton of employees who burn out quickly after hiring. What can *you* do to reach out to your team members enthusiastically and engage them?

- Maybe you're doing something wrong, and it's keeping you from hiring the best employees. What can you change to start attracting and retaining only the best?

When it comes to where we start and what we fix, this mindset is critical. In fact, we tell clients all the time that we're going to spend 70 percent of our time together working on the way we *think* about the people we hire. If you're thinking about people wrong, you will attract the wrong people.

Some of this might feel warm and fuzzy, very "hold hands around a campfire." But trust us that the investments you make up front by creating connections with your people are going to pay back endless dividends.

When you come into this process with a sense of what needs attention first and the mindset that *you* can fix it, the rest takes care of itself.

That's not to say implementation is easy. We've detailed the Core Fit Hiring System, but there's simply too much to this process to include every possible angle or situation. We understand, and we're here to help. You can contact us anytime—whether that's about getting things started, building the entire system, or troubleshooting a particular problem.

To access additional resources or contact us to learn more about how we can help you implement the process outlined in this book, visit us at https://hirebetterpeople-faster.com.

If you've gotten this far, you have what it takes to transform your organization. You can hire better people faster, and we're here to help you do that in any way we can.

ACKNOWLEDGMENTS

I want to give a massive shout-out to all the partners and clients who trusted me to guide them on their journey to hire better people faster. I wouldn't have your amazing stories to tell nor would I have been able to refine this process.

I also want to thank the people who have been in my corner through thick and thin: my mentors, friends, and colleagues who have supported and challenged me every step of the way.

A special thank-you to my dad. You instilled in me a work ethic that is incomparable and helped me to see what drove you to do so much for our family. I love you!

Thanks also to Tammy Eberhart for always having my back and making sure we're always improving—our process, service to our clients, and this book!

To Mike Toney, for your guidance and leadership—even when it was tough to hear. You inspired me to do more and be more.

And to Jeremy Macliver. Thank you for partnering with me on this book. It's a better book because of your contributions.

To my lovely and incredibly supportive wife, Elisha. You're my best friend and always there for me when the world knocks me down. Thank you for your love and support as I share this message with the world.

Thank you to all you amazing people for being a part of this journey and guiding me along the way.

And finally, to my Lord and Savior, Jesus Christ. You never said it would be easy, but you definitely made it worth it.

—**Ryan**

Writing a book is a massive undertaking, and just like running a business, there are a lot of unknowns that you need an expert on. When Ryan and I started on this, it was just a dream. It wouldn't be here without the help and support of the team that came together to support our cause. To each of you who contributed, test read, and guided us through this journey, I'm very thankful for your participation.

A million thanks to my favorite mom. Without you, I wouldn't be here, in more ways than one! Your writing inspired my love for writing. Your growth inspired my love for growth. And I would put a third thing here, because you always said it should be written in threes, but you know what I mean. I'm thankful for all that you taught me. And you too, Dad, thanks for always being there. Your confidence and wisdom mean a lot to me.

A special thanks to Katie Waldrup! You truly are the Director of my Chaos! Thanks for keeping me organized throughout the journey.

And to Ryan Englin. Thank you for partnering with me on this book. Your skill, attention to detail, and sheer tenacity to make this book the best book on hiring is impressive. It was an honor to work with you on this.

To my crazy family! My wife, Tina, and my kids, Jared, Lydia, Moriah, and Jeremiah. Your laughs at different cover designs, your thoughtful suggestions about different stories, and the one-liners you told your friends—"Yeah, my dad is writing another BBB...Boring Business Book." Thanks for your confidence and support.

Thank you to all you amazing people for being a part of this journey and guiding me along the way.

—Jeremy